# CRIME SCENE INVESTIGATION
# PUZZLE UNIT

Published in 2020 by Welbeck
An imprint of Welbeck Non-Fiction Limited,
part of Welbeck Publishing Group
20 Mortimer Street
London W1T 3JW

A CIP catalogue for this book is available from
the British Library.

ISBN 978-1-78739-448-3

Printed in Dubai

# CRIME SCENE INVESTIGATION
# PUZZLE UNIT

## 100 CRIMINALLY CHALLENGING PUZZLES TO SOLVE

JOEL JESSUP

WELBECK

# CONTENTS

DI DUSTIN AKSOY

DI JACK VERNON

DI ABIGAIL BECKHOFF

DI KELVIN KEMPSTER

# INTRODUCTION

Welcome to the CSI Puzzle Unit.

In this book you will step into the shoes of a police investigator who is after the trickiest quarry of all – the police themselves. Your task – codenamed Operation Barrow – will be explained further by CS Bill Stoneman. For now, you just need to know that it will be no routine investigation.

The book itself is split into 10 chapters, each detailing a particular case, and each with 10 puzzles of their own. Solve them all correctly, and you should have solved the case, too. However, you also have to pay close attention to your colleagues as you work. They all have their own secrets, and one of them just might be the traitor. The 100th and final puzzle will require you to name who you think is the corrupt cop in league with the criminal underworld.

The cases themselves are all solvable with a bit of ingenuity and perseverance. They are all of a similar difficulty level, although each case has a variety of degrees of difficulty within them; it is likely that one or two of the puzzles in each chapter will seem obvious to a practiced puzzler, but there will be at least one or two puzzles that will test the puzzling skills of everyone.

Similarly, some might require a level of general knowledge that you might not necessarily have. For example, you might need to know how certain pieces move in chess, in order to achieve a checkmate. In these instances, do not be afraid to search online for additional information that might help you. A good detective need not be like Sherlock Holmes, with all of the world's knowledge at their fingertips. Instead, they need to know the correct questions to ask in order to uncover all of the information they need to get to the truth.

Good luck and enjoy yourself. But remember, accuse the wrong colleague of corruption and not only will your cover be blown, but your career will be in tatters!

# CSI PUZZLE UNIT

# POLICE
## CSI PUZZLE UNIT

To: deaddrop73@secureserve.org.ch
From: CS.Bill.Stoneman@met.police.uk

Subject: Operation Barrow

Congratulations on getting the evidence on Thomas Price. May he rot in whatever nasty prison he gets thrown in.

Anyway, Operation Barrow. I'm sorry to saddle you with this but it's potentially an avalanche of trouble. And you are the Edmund Hillary of negotiating avalanches of trouble and climbing the mountain of success. Is that a bad metaphor? Who cares.

I'm sure you know about the Forensic Analysis Detective unit that's been operating inside SCD4 for about five years. Combining lab technicians together with detectives and Scene Of Crime Officers into one role in the hope it could cut down on the usual problems of people not seeing connections, blah, blah.

For the first four years, there's been no problems beyond the usual occasional slip-ups. But then we had a high-profile case fall through due to fundamental, easily missed errors. We took a look at some of their other cases and there are a few other places where things look a bit dodgy.

I think one of the detectives might be working for a criminal organization. From cross-referencing cases, we've narrowed it down to four possible infiltrators: DI Dustin Aksoy, DI Jack Vernon, DI Kevin Kempster and DI Abigail Beckhoff. We've set you up to join the unit; your past forensic training should enable you to fit in like a whippet up a pair of bellbottomed trousers. Work with them on their cases, analyze their behaviour, and for God's sake find me someone who's responsible for the entire mess. Otherwise we're going to have to shut the whole squad down and everything they've ever touched goes into review.

I don't want this giving me nightmares, right? I'm the only nightmare round here.

*Bill*

Bill

PA Upright

# BATTLE STATIONS

**Your first action** before you join the Forensic Analysis Detective team is to covertly look at their email accounts.

Abigail Beckhoff's emails are very professional, drafted like a report and following all official guidelines. You sense her working-class background makes her feel she has to try harder than the other detectives. No personal details. She received an email from her younger brother begging for help with some gambling debts but she never replied.

Jack Vernon's emails are sloppier. Nothing incriminating obviously, but you wouldn't expect the infiltrator to use an official email address to talk to his criminal bosses. Vernon prefers the lab to the field and you sense he would happily downgrade to being just a technician but, in the team, everyone does triple duty as a technician, detective and Scene of Crime Officer, or "SOCO".

Kelvin Kempster's emails are similar to Beckhoff's but much chattier. His father was a Detective Superintendent so he's quite well connected. He's clearly interested in making friends to help his career but he's just as hard-working as the other detectives. Sometimes he seems uncertain about his conclusions, but collaboration is important in science.

However, it's Dustin Aksoy's emails that surprise and initially worry you the most. Aksoy is the oldest member of the team but behaves like the youngest, sending dozens of emails to everyone on subjects from new blood-analysis tools to the latest sci-fi blockbuster to tabletop war games. Aksoy loves pop culture and joking around, and if it wasn't for his considerable skill both in the lab and the field, he would probably have been fired already.

Your concern comes from noticing he has some encrypted emails going to an unknown third party, and when you use a key program to decode the unsophisticated cypher he's using, you find lists of weapons, some of which sound like those used in the field of war, although some of them are listed as lasers and plasma swords. They're also said to be plastic, although maybe that's to help them get through metal detectors?

There's also a detailed description of troop movements – although the distances marked seem to be in centimetres rather than kilometres – and a reference to "The Coming Storm", which is said to be "out of this world!" Furthermore, there are invoices that show considerable amounts of money changing hands in a regular pattern and, strangely, a lot of orders for tiny pots of paint.

DI ABIGAIL BECKHOFF

*** SPAM *** IT TRAINING SCHOLARSHIPS

DI JACK VERNON

*** SPAM *** IT TRAINING SCHOLARSHIPS

DI KELVIN KEMPSTER

*** SPAM *** IT TRAINING SCHOLARSHIPS

DI DUSTIN AKSOY

*** SPAM *** IT TRAINING SCHOLARSHIPS

## Why has Aksoy sent these emails?

Solution on page 196

# OUR CUNNING DETECTIVE

**Aksoy gets the call:** a man has been found battered to death in a small bedsit in Acton. Aksoy is excited when he's told no one has been witnessed entering or leaving the room during the time the murder must have occurred. The body was found by his landlady, who then called the police repeatedly. "An actual locked-room mystery!" he enthuses. "Strap on your skates, Watson!"

On the way to the scene, he's even more excited when he realizes who the victim was. "Jan Holub! The chess grandmaster! He's been off the circuit for decades now but he was a pretty big deal in the eighties. The bad boy of chess!"

Whatever success he may have had in the past, Holub evidently either didn't profit or didn't save anything, because his bedsit is a tiny two-room affair at the top of a rickety set of stairs in an old Victorian townhouse that had been divided into four tiny residences.

"Check out these steps!" says Aksoy with wonder as you negotiate the twisty old staircase. "It's a wonder he didn't slip and break his neck years ago. Especially if you look at how scrubbed and varnished they are."

In fact, the whole corridor is scrupulously cleaned to such an extent it almost looks like a film set.

At the top of the stairs, you pause in the cramped corridor to pull on your protective suits. The PC on guard gives you both a friendly nod. Next to him is the landlady, a tiny Eastern European woman in her mid-to-late thirties. She looks very tense and is compulsively straightening and smoothing her dress. Aksoy may have his faults but he immediately tries to put her at ease, although it has no noticeable effect.

The room is cramped and musty and has packed about three houses' worth of a life

into two rooms. Lots of mementoes and photos stand in perfect alignment. Framed awards are piled on a table in the corner in order of size. At the centre lies his scruffily dressed body, crumpled over, head wound covered in now darkening blood. In the centre of the room is a beaten-up old table, at the centre of which is an antique-looking chess set with a game already in progress. Just visible underneath the table is a brick-shaped chess clock, seemingly knocked to the floor.

However, Aksoy puts his hand up. "My Dustin-sense is tingling. Severe head trauma could indicate a crime of passion, yes. But someone has cleaned and tidied this scene post-mortem."

The room's central light suddenly goes off, then on, then off again. Everyone's eyes suddenly turn to the landlady, who is flicking the light switch repeatedly. You throw a look at Aksoy. The murderer?

Aksoy shakes his head and smiles. "I think there's a simpler explanation."

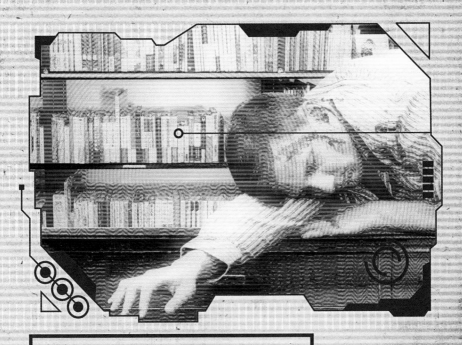

## Who cleaned the room and why?

Solution on page 196

# BIRD'S OPENING

**DI Aksoy decides** to check Mr Holub's ancient-looking computer for information. But instead of a password, it presents a puzzle with images.

Kingfisher | Raven | Yellow bishop | Rook | Nightjar

## Which bird is the odd one out?

Solution on page 196

# QUIZ TIME

**Now the chess grandmaster's** computer brings up a series of questions. The answers lead Aksoy to a realization about who might be the murderer.

1. What two plumbers are known for wearing red and green and jumping on turtles?

2. "Bye Love" is a song from 1957 sung by which country-influenced rock'n'roll duo from Kentucky?

3. Name the overseeing force in George Orwell's classic book *1984*.

4. Which film directed by the Coen Brothers stars George Clooney as an escaped convict in 1937 Mississippi?

5. Who were famous for collecting and popularizing folk tales such as *Cinderella*, *The Frog Prince* and *Hansel and Gretel*?

## What is the connection between all the answers?

Solution on page 196

# ON A LINE OF INQUIRY

**Deciding to question the** landlady because she found the body, Aksoy listens sombrely to her dramatic description of discovering the corpse at 7 a.m. that morning, as the man would usually pay her the rent in cash on the 12th of each month. The landlady keeps looking at her phone, and you reason she might be receiving messages or trying to calm herself.

"I can't believe Jan's gone; he was one of my best friends," she muttered. "He would always tell me about his time back in Czechoslovakia, in... Bratislava with his little friends, running around."

"Do any of his friends live nearby?"

"Just a minute..." she said, then continued, "He had his rock band, Black is White... Oh, but they broke up in 1990! His father is, err... dead. Oh, he was almost *Time* magazine's man of the year in 1977 but they went with Anwar Sadat..."

"What about his brother? Did he have any contact?"

"It doesn't say. I mean, he... he didn't say. We didn't talk much. Uh, about his brother, I mean. But a lot about everything else. Did you know..."

The usefulness of this is starting to evade you, but Aksoy is happy to nod along until she says her phone battery has died and toddles off to plug it in.

"Considering their closeness, she's still a big suspect, I think..." you suggest.

"She didn't know him from Adamski!" Aksoy said. "Or even Anwar Sadat. I think if she passed him on the street she wouldn't have recognized him."

"Then how did she know so much about him?"

"Easy."

## Why does she know so much about Jan Holub?

Solution on page 196

# CYTOSINE, GUANINE, ADENINE AND THYMINE

**Back at the lab,** you take the samples of DNA that Aksoy gathered from the scene and match them with samples from the body and the landlady to find if there are any discrepancies.

DEPARTMENT NAME _____

00510450

RECEIPT NO. _____ RECEIVED BY _____ DATE _____
(SIGNATURE)

00510450

(TO BE OPENED BY AUTHORIZED PERSONNEL ONLY)

```
C C T T G A A C T T C T G T A T C G
C G A G G G A T A G C C A T T G G C
G A T C G T T C C G T C T T A T G C
T A G T T C G A A T A C A G C C A G
C A G C G A T T A C G T T A G A T C
C T C G G T G T C A A C T T A G C T
A C A C C A C T C C G A T G A C G A
G G T A G T A C T A A G A C G C A T
G C C C T C C G A A G T C G T A T T
A C C T C C T A G C G A C T A G C G
T T G T C T A C C A G T A T C C T G
C T A T T G G T A C A A T T A C T C
G G T A T A G C A A G T C C G T A G
C A C C T A T G A G T T G A A C T T
T G C C G G G G T T A G A C G A C C
T G C A A G A T G A C G G A A A G G
A C G A A T C C A C T A A T T G C C
G A C T G C A T A C T C C A C C T G
```

| | |
|---|---|
| CCTCCGAAGTC | TACGAAGTA |
| GTGCACTAGGT | ATACAGCCA |
| CATGGTTA | AGGGATAGC |
| CCGATCCC | GATCGATC |
| AGTTGAAC | TGACGGA |

Solution on page 197

# MAKE LIKE A TREE

**After talking to** the other residents in the building, you and Aksoy realize that the victim was basically a hermit, rarely seen outside of his room. This makes the question of who killed him even more mysterious. "It's not a locked-room mystery, it's a locked-life mystery! This'll be really good for..." begins Aksoy, then he suddenly goes quiet. "Never mind."

Taking the landlady's actions as inspiration, he goes online and finds a biography about Jan Holub, titled *My Life, One Square At A Time*. Rather than trying to speed read the whole manuscript, he connects with the author on Twitter and has a five-minute chat about Holub's friends and family.

"OK, this is what he told me," says Aksoy, as he gathers some trace evidence. "Holub was loud and proud all over the chess scene until 1995 when he got beat by Vladimir Akopian in a 'friendly' match. No one's sure what rattled him so much but he disappeared. He must have had a fair chunk of cash but his present dwelling suggests that didn't last. No noticeable friends in the area. Akopian lives in Armenia and doesn't strike me as a violent murderer. And his family... Well..."

Aksoy takes a deep breath.

"He had a brother, Jozef, who was also trained in chess at the same time as him but crashed out. He was a businessman for a time but got caught embezzling in 2004 – disappeared off to Brazil probably. His dad, Milan, also a grandmaster but not on the same level, really, remarried a woman named Anna after Jan's mother, Jana, died. With Anna, he had two more sons: Tomáš and Adam. Then he divorced her and married her sister, Helena, and adopted her daughter, Martina. Then – get this – the adopted daughter's daughter, also named Jana, married the son of one of his father's other sons. His name is Miroslav – the son of Adam, I mean, not the son of the son – and this kid, Peter, is Jan's closest living relative! He's in Muswell Hill, actually. Works as a butcher."

You give Aksoy a sceptical look and he shrugs. "Well, that's how the biographer told it to me," he says.

## Questions

1. What relation is Anna to the victim?
2. What relation is the second Jana to the victim?
3. What relation is Peter to the victim?

Solution on page 197

# UPTOWN TOP RANKING

**Aksoy is back in the victim's room**, looking at the objects inside like a tourist at a Jan Holub exhibition. But his record means you don't mistake his excitement for distraction. He gets a message on his phone and then turns to you with excitement.

"I got Vernon to check out the landlady's credentials and – get this – she doesn't actually own the building; it's owned by some company called Knight Enterprises, and guess what Holub's other nickname was? The Black Knight of Chess! Corny, I know, but do you think he owned the whole house? Why did he live like this then? Was he punishing himself?"

Aksoy looks at the chess game and smiles.

"I think this is the key. Nothing missing in the room; nothing stolen. But there's this game and, unless Mr Holub was playing against himself, it takes two, baby. So they're playing and then WHAM! The other player hits poor old Jan right on the top of his head. With what?"

Aksoy gets down, with the game at his eye level.

"One of the knights is missing. Taken as a memento? Hmm. We'll have to find that. And something else is missing too!"

He indicates a rectangular-shaped absence of dust on the surface of the table right next to the board.

"Your turn, detective. What would any professional chess player have right here?" he asks you, playfully. "You see them all the 'time'…" But before he answers his own question, he suddenly spots something else in the room.

"Wow! Really?" he says to himself.

Aksoy now starts carefully stepping around the room, heel-to-toe, as if measuring it with his feet.

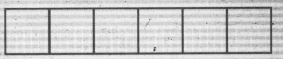

"The walls are a strangely irregular length for such a standard room design. One, two, three, four, I spy… a hidden door!" he shouts as he reaches one of the bookshelves and pulls down on one of the books theatrically.

Nothing happens. He pulls a few more books and then shrugs.

"I guess they're not triggers. However…"

He pulls the entire shelf away from the wall to reveal a poster advertising a chess match between Holub – "The Black Knight" – and his brother, who is called "Scarface".

"They called him that because his birthday was on Valentine's Day," Aksoy says. "And he was born exactly forty years after the St Valentine's Day Massacre in 1929. It's not a good nickname, really."

He gestures around the poster and you can see how it hides the lines of a hidden door.

"Shall we just knock, or…"

Inlaid further down is a smaller outline, and pushing against it allows Aksoy to slide a panel to the left, revealing a number pad, much more sophisticated than the clunky nineties reject computer already occupying the room. Kneeling down and squinting at it, Aksoy grins and shakes his head. "Looks like it's puzzle time again."

The small display screen has enough room for six numbers, and has a little image of a cake with candles on it.

"What do you think?" Aksoy asks.

# What is the number you need to put into the keypad?

Solution on page 197

# HEAD MASTER

**Aksoy gets a call from** DI Kempster, who has been running scans of Holub's head back at the lab. They reveal massive blunt trauma. But was it caused by the fall or something else found in the room, as shown in the grid below?

Based on the nature of impact, what is the most likely murder weapon? Is there anything else that may have contributed to his death?

Solution on page 197

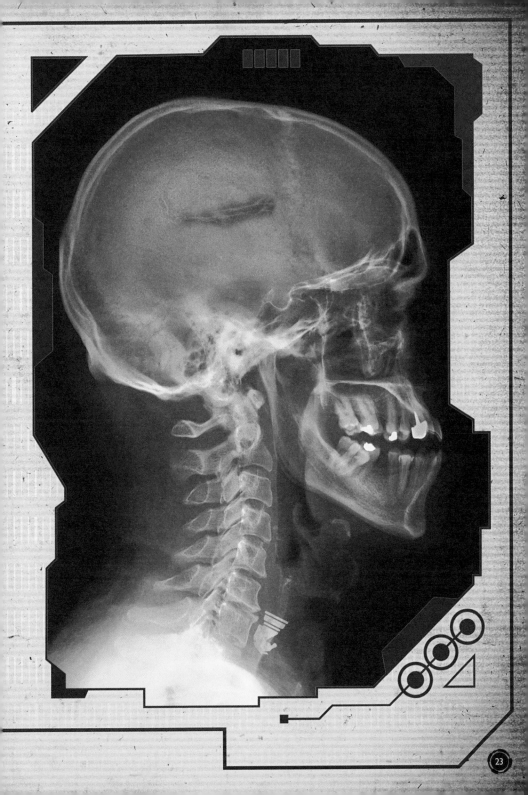

# ŠACH – MAT

**The door slides open** to reveal a slightly more spacious living area, with a built-in kitchen and other doors, no doubt linking to adjoining bedrooms and a bathroom. Sitting on an overstuffed sofa, looking rather sheepish, is an old man with red-rimmed eyes.

"Jozef Holub, I presume?" says Aksoy, in a neutral tone.

The old man nods his head, and looks like he's going to cry.

"Have you really lived in this cubby hole since 2004?" Aksoy asks, as the police officers who have accompanied you file into the room behind you, peering around with amazement.

"No, no, I have travelled around, but then I made a few mistakes, and Jan offered to put me up here about two years ago. He made it especially. I thought he had forgiven our quarrels, but…" Jozef shook his head sadly, then continued. "Jan was only interested in playing chess. He has never beaten me, and he just wanted to play again and again. Just like when we were kids, me versus him, Black versus White. Every time I asked that we take a break, he threatened to expose me to the authorities. I was trapped here. I considered escape, but the landlady would see me. You know, she has a photographic memory; she would definitely recognize and report me."

Solution on page 198

He sits down at the chess table. "Then, you know, it happened – he beat me. He was so excited he grabbed the knight I had taken previously and kissed it, but then he... swallowed it somehow. When he began choking, I tried to help but he fought me off. Then, when he fell, his head hit the clock..." He stops talking and looks down at the board. His face turns furious.

"The pieces are back in place. But he knocked them over when he fell! And... they're wrong. I don't understand. Wasn't his knight...? That hajzel is trying to cheat me, even in death!"

Aksoy nods at one of the PCs and they grab and cuff Jozef before he gets more violent.

"I think his reaction tells us a lot. The only thing he had over Jan was his chess skills, and when Jan finally wins a match, it's too much for Jozef, and down comes the clock on Jan's genius head, followed by a chess piece for dessert. Then he tries to wait it all out in the secret room, maybe go on the run again once we've left."

It sounds plausible. But...

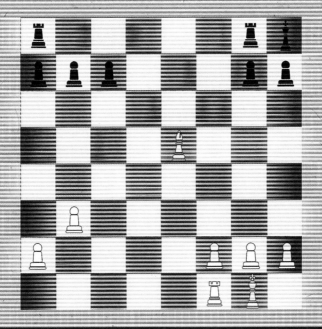

# 1. How did the pieces get back on the board?
# 2. What is wrong or out of place with the arrangement of the pieces?

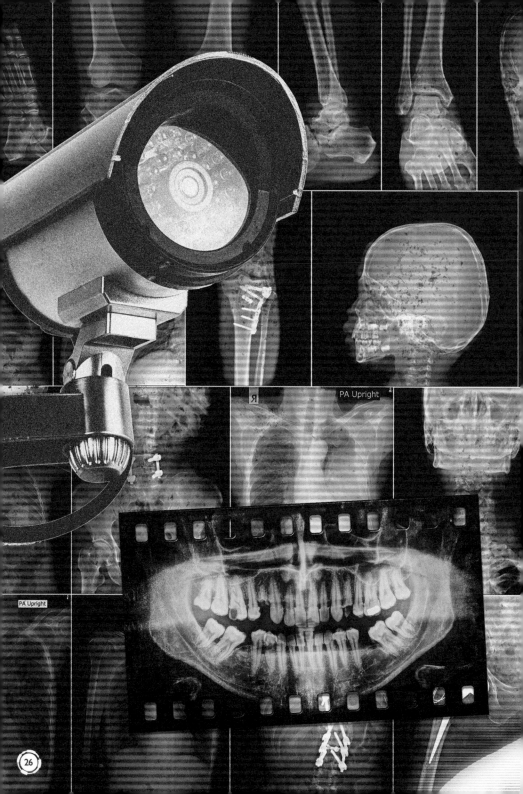

PA Upright

PA Upright

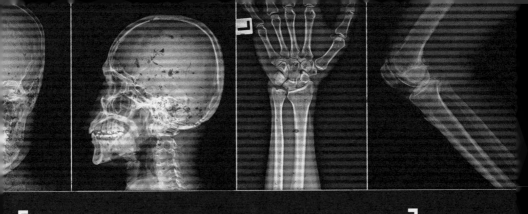

# CSI CHAPTER 2:
# FIRE DOWN BELOW

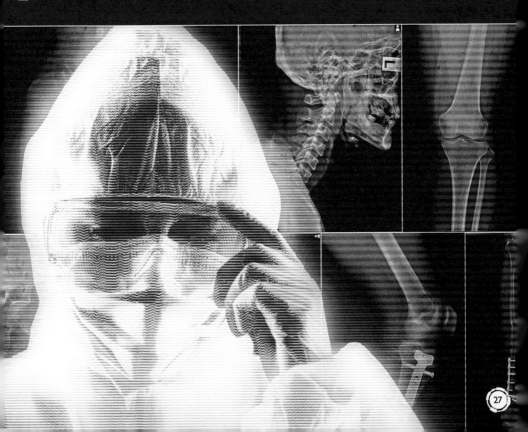

# MY COUSIN VINCENT

**Aksoy is talking to you** about the plot of a sci-fi movie that you're sure hasn't actually come out yet when he gets a message.

"Huh. Fire Brigade Investigation Unit. They want us to have a look at a suspicious blaze over in a chip shop in Woolwich. They think there might be criminal intent."

"Aren't they already set up to investigate those things?"

"Short story, yes, but there's some confusing elements."

When you arrive at the shop, it's already cordoned off. The chip shop, called Whitechapel Fried Chicken, doesn't look too damaged from the outside, but once you put on your protective suits and enter, the effect of the blaze is more evident, with a small group of Fire Brigade Investigators taking samples from all round the dishevelled and fire-damaged shop. It looks like a standard chicken-and-chip shop, glass-fronted counters and deep-fat fryers lying dormant. One of the men waves you and Aksoy over.

"Meet Bob Kyriacou of the FBI!" says Aksoy merrily.

"Don't call us the FBI," says Bob with the deadpan expression of someone used to dealing with Aksoy. "The real action is downstairs. Lots of 'alligatoring' – you know, that cracked pattern on the wall. Five bodies. Looks like they were boozing and smoking in the shop's storage area, a stray match or spliff gets dropped, and KABOOM! Lots of flammables down there."

"But?" asks Aksoy.

"But, the fire's point of origin is not near the bodies, so we think possible criminal intent."

"What about the owner?"

Bob points to a spot outside where a tearful looking man, balding, mid-fifties, is being questioned by one of the investigators.

"Dan Tipton. This is one of a few shops he owns in London, but he works from here, apparently. ID'd the victims. They're his cousin, Vincent Tipton, and four other young people: all employees."

Aksoy walks down the scorched concrete steps to the basement crime scene while you wander over to Mr Tucker.

"I tell you, I never heard nothing like that sound before. That's why I didn't do nothing at first. I mean, you don't think stuff is going to explode, do you? I mean, I done this fire safety course, but this was something else!"

"What time did you hear the explosion?" you ask.

"Well, actually, there was two, I reckon!" he says. "I put a batch of chips on and heard this weird sort of thud noise. Didn't sound like an explosion at first, then about when the chips were done about thirty minutes later, I heard this much louder woomf noise – the place shook! Once the smoke started coming out, I got me and all the customers out on the street quick as I could. I thought about going in, but I know all about smoke inhalation and that."

You step away from the man and head toward the scene. His story seems to provide him with an alibi… except one detail bothers you.

**What details suggests the man might be lying about his whereabouts?**

Solution on page 198

# BODY HEAT

**You enter the basement.** It's a heat-blasted pit, the walls pitch black from smoke. Aksoy is already kneeling in some ash. He is taking pictures on his phone.

"No reception down here. I'll email you the pics later. The bodies are in the morgue, basically charcoal briquettes. But I'm sure you can figure out where they were."

Fill in the grid so that each of the body parts are placed correctly. The numbers along the rows and columns tell you how many body parts in total are in that row or column. No two different body parts may touch, even diagonally. No body parts are present where there is an oil barrel.

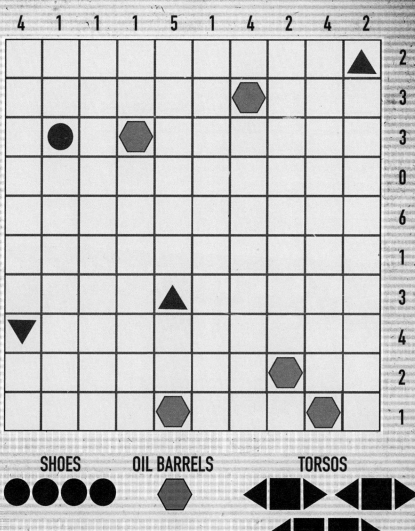

|   | 4 | 1 | 1 | 1 | 5 | 1 | 4 | 2 | 4 | 2 |
|---|---|---|---|---|---|---|---|---|---|---|
| 2 |   |   |   |   |   |   |   |   |   | ▲ |
| 3 |   |   |   |   |   |   | ⬡ |   |   |   |
| 3 |   | ● |   | ⬡ |   |   |   |   |   |   |
| 0 |   |   |   |   |   |   |   |   |   |   |
| 6 |   |   |   |   |   |   |   |   |   |   |
| 1 |   |   |   |   |   |   |   |   |   |   |
| 3 |   |   |   |   | ▲ |   |   |   |   |   |
| 4 | ▼ |   |   |   |   |   |   |   |   |   |
| 2 |   |   |   |   |   |   |   | ⬡ |   |   |
| 1 |   |   |   |   | ⬡ |   |   |   | ⬡ |   |

**SHOES**

**OIL BARRELS**

**TORSOS**

**LIMBS**

**FULL BODY**

Solution on page 198

# BITE-SIZED

**Aksoy heads back to the lab**, where they've delivered him a nice surprise: one of the barbecued corpses, this one barely more than a skeleton with bits of burned meat.

"Apparently, this is the only one they couldn't ID. Could be a hanger on, or it could be our arsonist. Cooked his own goose."

You don't laugh.

Aksoy brings a bunch of dental records up on the big screen. "Shouldn't be too difficult to find a match. These are the three most likely candidates."

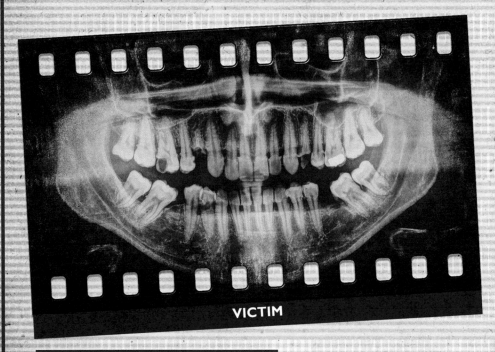

VICTIM

## Whose dental records match the corpse's teeth?

Solution on page 199

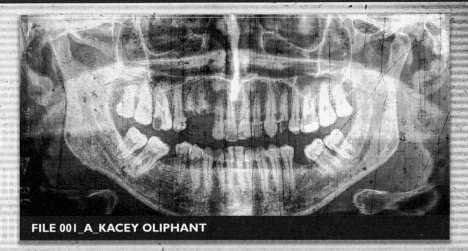

FILE 001_A_KACEY OLIPHANT

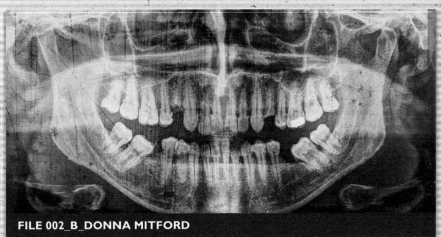

FILE 002_B_DONNA MITFORD

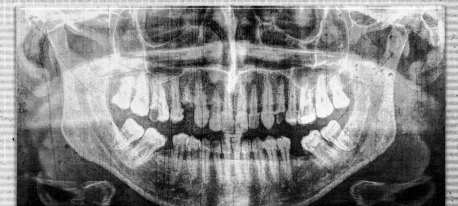

FILE 003_C_TIM BALDACCI

# BURNT OFFERINGS

**Bob Kyriacou sends over** some high-quality images of the burned items they found in the basement. Looking at the remains, you realise that one of them is definitely a little out of place.

## Which item is the odd one out and had no use being in the basement?

Solution on page 199

# INVESTIGATING UNITS

**Aksoy looks unusually annoyed.** "OK, so far everything about this just suggests a standard stoner party gone wrong. I'm not really seeing a criminal-intent rap here. And get this: the owner, Tipton? No insurance. So there would be no benefit for him to torch the place."

Aksoy sits down and takes a look at the image of broken bottles Kyriacou has sent him.

"Maybe, if we figure out how drunk they were, we can see if they were capable of this."

You look at the scene report. Vincent Tipton was holding a half-empty beer bottle and had four more empty bottles next to him. Tim Baldacci was holding a shot glass. There was an empty vodka bottle next to him and a half-empty whisky bottle between him and Yasmin Satrapi. She wasn't holding a glass, but was holding an empty wine box. Monica Satrapi, her sister, was "supposed" to be a teetotaller according to Tipton, but she had an empty half-size bottle of 80 per cent absinthe in her hand! Ben Jackson had two empty bottles of Châteauneuf-du-Pape, no less, but it seems likely they would all have had some of that, even if they were just swigging from the bottle.

You know that one alcohol unit is 10 ml or 8 g of pure alcohol. A whiskey or vodka bottle is 40 units, a beer bottle is 1.7 units and a wine bottle is typically 10 units. A wine box has the equivalent of 4 bottles of wine in it. A shot of absinthe is equivalent to a bottle of beer, and there's 30 shots in a bottle.

## Assuming that what they had is what they drank, how many units did each of them consume?

Solution on page 199

# OUT OF HIS SKULL

**Aksoy ponders the results.** "Holy wine, they were all loaded. Except, perhaps, for Ben. Plus, they were all smoking weed. Do we know who brought it?"

Tipton's statement says he thought Ben might have been dealing but he had no evidence. He saw someone selling around the corner from him wearing one of those skull-face bandanas. There's a gang that operates near him. He thinks Ben's a member of it but, again, no evidence! Here's what we do know:

1. No member of this gang heading to a major purchase ever fails to carry a concealed pistol.

2. In my experience, gang members are always calm under pressure if they're reliable.

3. Tipton never thought Ben had any self-control; he was definitely reckless.

4. The gang members are only allowed a concealed pistol if they can prove they're always calm under pressure.

5. They only wear the skull-face bandanas if they're going to a major purchase – it's like a signal.

6. The gang members are always unreliable if they have no self-control.

REC

Does Ben ever wear skull-face bandanas?

Solution on page 199

# WHERE ARE THE MOLECULES?

**Aksoy takes one of the pieces** of fire debris. Inserting a special head-space syringe into its sealed plastic bag, he draws out a sample of vapour. He crosses the room and injects the vapour directly into a Gas Chromatograph Mass Spectrometer (GC-MS) that occupies a rather crowded corner of his personal work area.

"Sorry, a lot of this stuff was in room 14A but we had to clear out of there – structural problems, apparently."

He activates the device and it quickly separates out the components and analyzes and monitors the contents for the specific types of typical accelerants used in arson cases: gasoline, kerosene, other inflammable liquids. Pretty soon, the screen displays the results. Aksoy whistles.

| | | |
|---|---|---|
| BUTANE | GASOLINE | KEROSENE |
| OXYGEN | CARBON DIOXIDE | WATER |

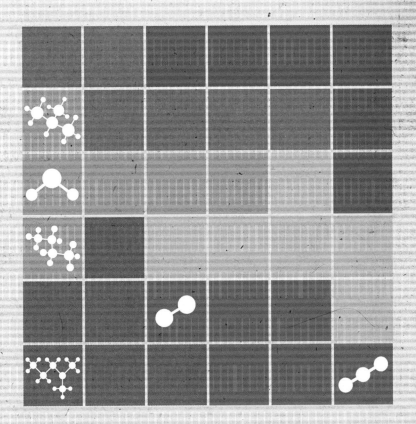

To recreate the results from the GC-MS, you must make sure that there is no more than one of each thing in each column and row, and that nothing of the same type are adjacent to one another. The molecule in row 1, column 5 was shown to be present on the scene.

Solution on page 200

# RATTED OUT

**The presence of kerosene cinches it:** this must have been arson. Mindful of the fact that there may be undiscovered forensic evidence in the shop, rather than the basement, you and Aksoy return to the scene. Outside, the owner, Tipton, is arguing with Bob Kyriacou.

"I need to assess the damage, mate. I mean, if I'm going to have any chance of salvaging the equipment…"

"Sorry, you can't go in. It's an ongoing investigation."

Suddenly, you hear a loud squeaking noise. All four of you simultaneously turn your head to see a very bold-looking rat gazing up at you. You all stand frozen for a long while, before it comes sprinting at you. Instinctively, you leap out of the way, while Tipton darts his foot out to kick at it, hissing.

"Shoo, shoo!"

The rat leaps away, but despite Tipton's best efforts, it keeps trying to enter the shop.

"See what I have to deal with? Bloody vermin!"

After a moment of hesitation, Aksoy advances towards it and, to your intense shock, picks it up! It starts nuzzling his hand. He brings it over to you to examine. It has grey fur, with white and brown blotches, and is about 12 inches long. There is a thin mark around the fur on its neck but otherwise it looks just like any other rat as far as you are concerned, not that you generally examine them too closely.

"I knew it! It's someone's pet — I'd bet all my space marines on it. An old girlfriend used to have one. If it turns out not to have anything to do with the case, at least we'll be doing something for animal welfare."

As he continues to play with the rat, you dial the number for the RSPCA.

## How did Aksoy know that it was a domesticated rat before he picked it up?

Solution on page 200

# SPARK OUT

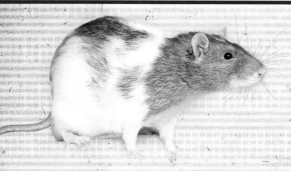

An RSPCA officer arrives to take custody of the rat, and promises to get Aksoy its details soon. Once they leave, Aksoy heads back into the crime scene, past a still-complaining Tipton, and examines the shop area. After looking for evidence of trace amounts of accelerant or other materials, he instead finds a lone potato, which he stares at with joy.

"Look at this – little one-centimetre nibbles taken out of it. The rat definitely fed on this."

You see he's right; there is a series of tiny little gouges.

Then he notices a plug with a long lead that goes into the wall.

"What's this for, I wonder. It's not the fryers or any other equipment. I think it leads into the basement."

Following the trail back into the blackened pit of the basement, he finds the wire leading down the stairs, seemingly pulled away from the wall.

"It's funny: this should be a bit melted and blackened from the fire," says Aksoy, following it down. In the basement, the wire connects to something hidden in a covered-over alcove – something that looks like a hot plate.

"Look at this! This is ancient. Maybe they used to cook down here."

Further examination of the wire shows that it is stripped of its plastic cover in one area, with a big, clean triangular chunk of approximately 5 cm taken out of it. There are no other bites anywhere on the entire length of the wire.

"Oh dear, this looks pretty dangerous. Maybe our little rat friend decided to have a nibble and then the spark from the exposed wire caused the fire. All they needed was to spill some of the flammable liquid down here. Or maybe even some of the spirits would have done it."

Aksoy stands back then, thoughtfully takes out a little swab and gets a sample from around the bites. Just as he finishes, his phone beeps. "Yep, RSPCA found a chip in our rat friend. His name is… Brocamoo? And he was owned by Vincent. So it's a little strange that the chip-shop owner didn't recognize the rat. I don't know: maybe I'm thinking about it too much. Apparently, it's completely unharmed."

Aksoy stands and looks at the scene.

"So the staff of this shop come down here for a sneaky late-night drinking session. They each consume a vast amount of alcohol, smoke some of that popular 'Mary Jane' the kids seem to like, generally mess around. Vincent, cousin of the owner, has brought his pet rat who, after having a bit of potato, decides to take a big, juicy bite out of the cable, gets a shock, spark ignites the petrol or whatever… this place is very flammable and it goes up like a roman candle."

Aksoy looks at you and raises an eyebrow. "What do you think of that theory?"

## What details confirm or discredit Aksoy's theory?

Solution on page 200

# DOWN WITH THE SICKNESS

**Back at the lab,** Aksoy is scrutinizing photos of the wire, eating a piece of toast. He holds the toast up in front of him, then compares it to the photo. "I think the bite marks were not from our little furry friend. What sort of animal would bite through an electrical cord?"

He waves the result of another test at you. "The autopsies show that any fire damage happened AFTER death. No coal pigment was observed in the mucosa of the upper airways at autopsy, so they weren't breathing. Maybe they all had alcohol poisoning. Let's test the bottles."

Aksoy takes vapour samples from the empty drinking vessels found at the crime scene and runs them through the GC-MS. The results are not only shocking but highly illuminating. "I don't recognize this compound. Let me check the database. Ipecac?"

Aksoy shakes his head, making notes. "Vomit city. Ipecac in the booze is a seriously powerful emetic. Could it have been a prank? Our drug-dealing friend trying to put them off the alcohol so he could sell them more weed? That seems unlikely, as they seemed to put away a lot of it."

DI Beckhoff, stopping in to talk to Aksoy about the case, has some expertise in this area: "Ipecac used to be recommended as an emergency treatment if people ingested poison, but it's longer recommended, largely because its purgative abilities didn't help and, in some quantities, it is itself a poison. It's an extract from the carapichea ipecacuanha plant... I did toxicology at college."

Aksoy nods. "In that case, I find it pretty unlikely that any of these youngsters thought 'Ooh, let's drink some ipecac for a joke.' Unless there's some kind of ipecac challenge on YouTube."

Beckhoff rolls her eyes and leaves the room. In the corner of the room, a tone informs Aksoy that the sample he took from the wire has been processed.

"No rat DNA. Just metallic particles. Looks like steel. Matches the profile of one of the burned objects. I think we should bring Tipton in."

Dan Tipton is deposited in one of the interrogation suites. He is sullen, grumbling that he should be tending his herb garden and that the rat chewed the wires.

Before you go in to question him, Aksoy takes you aside. "We managed to get data from one of the phones on the bodies. A group message: 'Dumb Dan closing the shop early, meet you in the basement.' So we need to hit him with all the evidence we've gathered. If we can get a confession, it'll be ideal because the fire, as it does, has complicated everything. Just think about the following: the accelerant, the ipecac, the age of the partiers and of Tipton, the rat, the chunk out of the wire, the steel we found and the burned objects."

*Cephaelis Ipecacuanha*

## 1. How did the people in the basement die?
## 2. Why did they die?
## 3. And what started the fire?

Solution on page 201

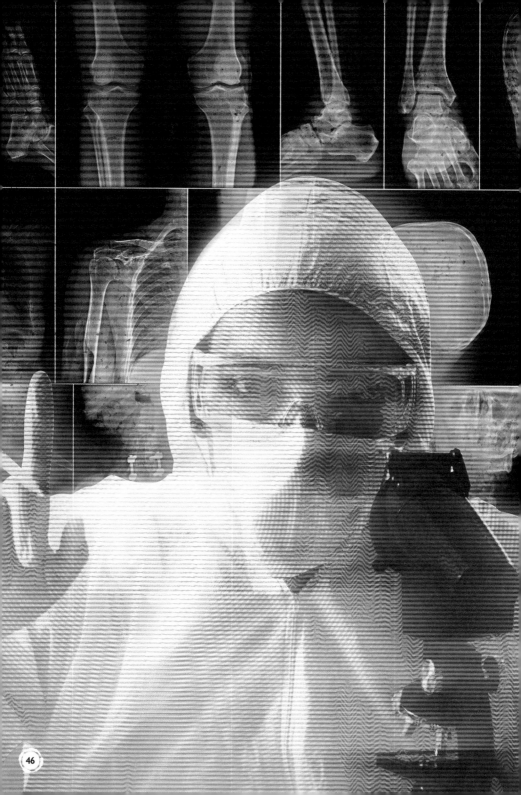

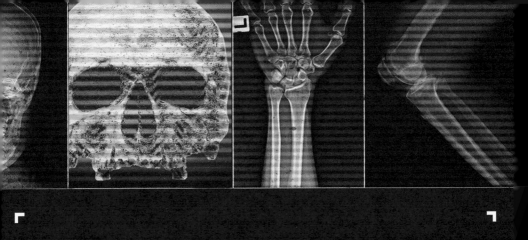

# CSI CHAPTER 3:
# WHAT LARKS

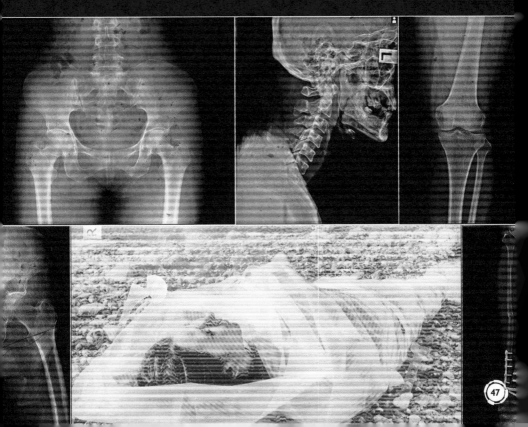

# OUT OF ORDER

**For a day or so**, you help DI Dustin Aksoy do busy work for other detective's cases. Once, you catch him making case notes in a separate notebook marked "DEV RESEARCH", but he hides it quickly.

Then a call comes in: a body has been found on the banks of the Thames in Wapping. They want Aksoy on the scene immediately before the tide washes away crucial evidence.

"Normally, a river bank would be an easy scene to close off, but since that mud-larking book came out everyone is traipsing around down there looking for old clocks or something."

You point out if it wasn't for that the body might never have been found. He shrugs agreement, and then sees the man who discovered the body.

"Ah, yes, I can tell you it was a bit of a shock, but it must be a recent corpse I found because it has begun the first stage of post-death: the rigor mortis…"

Solution on page 201

e man keeps talking, you realize he's got the stages of post-death in
letely the wrong order…

Rigor Mortis: corpse's limbs become stiff and hard to manipulate.

Decomposition: corpse reduces to simpler forms of matter, resulting in a strong, nasty smell.

Pallor Mortis: the skin becomes very pale.

Livor Mortis: as time passes, blood settles in the lower parts of the body due to the effects of gravity.

5. Algor Mortis: the body temperature reduces steadily until it reaches ambient temperature.

6. Skeletonization: all soft tissues have decomposed, leaving only the skeleton.

7. Putrefaction: early signs of the body decomposing.

Put these post-mortem stages in the correct order.

# REAR WINDOW(S)

**Directly by the river** is a former warehouse now converted into a block of flats. Five storeys high, you wonder whether anyone could have witnessed anything from there. All the windows are uncovered except for the fourth floor's very dusty-looking blinds.

You head up a rather tall and dubious set of wooden stairs and a protective row of iron railings that also look rather loose and rusty. A large crowd stands at the top — apparently, the flat's residents all craning for a look. They surge forwards to offer their "statements".

## Of these five statements, whose is believable?

"Is it a body? Must have fallen down the stairs," says an elderly lady.

"It wasn't the stairs – look at the mud! He was in the river; he was swimming backstroke in a pink bathing costume. I saw him," says a bearded man.

"From the ground floor?" asks a man in a dressing gown. "Unlikely. I was on the third floor. I was doing yoga at 5 a.m. and I saw a figure drag something there."

"Not dragged. He was hit by lightning! I saw it from the first floor," says a tiny lady in a hat.

"You have no line of sight on this beach," insists a man with big eyebrows. "I, on the fourth floor, saw clearly that the man was beset by seven or eight youths. In golfing outfits. With cricket bats."

"No, Bill's right. It was just one person that dragged the body onto the beach," says a man cradling a small racing pigeon.

"How did you see it?" asks the bearded man. "Your flat's on the other side!"

The other man lifts his pigeon up as if in response. "I was on the roof."

Solution on page 201

# INSECTS ASIDE

**Returning to the crime scene**, you find Aksoy carefully examining the body while singing a Beatles song under his breath.

"This dude is practically an insect zoo! You know Execution Dock is near here? It was a shoreline gallows, about two hundred-ish years ago — all sorts of wrong-uns and ne'er-do-wells would be hanged, and they'd leave their bodies to have three tides wash over them."

Aksoy stands up. "But I'll tell you what they wouldn't get: insect larvae. The Thames has mayflies, caddis flies, dragonflies, but their nymphs live entirely underwater — they'd never survive. So this changes our story somewhat. Take a look at what's on him. If we can figure out the insects and where they are in their life cycle, we'll have an idea of when and where he was murdered."

Calliphoridae —
Blow flies

Muscidae —
House flies

Hermetia illucens —
Black soldier fly

Sarcophagidae —
Flesh flies

The number of each type of fly found on the body is equal to the value the image of the fly represents in the below grid. Solve it to find out the amount of each type of fly that is present.

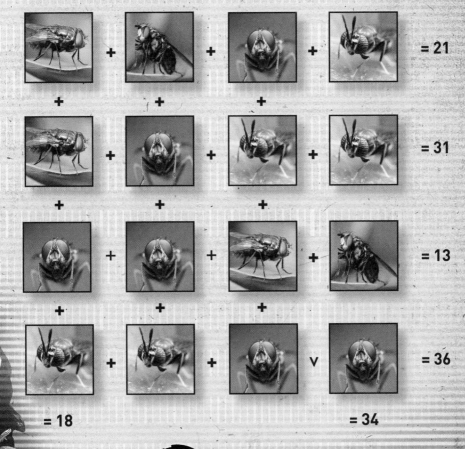

= 18

= 34

Solution on page 201

**You see another onlooker** standing right next to the tape. An officer is already going over to tell this nosey person to go away, but there's something in the woman's expression that strikes you as interesting so you walk over.

"Can I help you, madam?" you ask.

"Was walking Hogan and saw you'd set up over here. This isn't an MPF operation, is it?"

Marine Police Force, in other words.

"We're working with them, obviously, but can I ask your interest?"

"I just thought, this close to the MSU…" she says, using the acronym for the Marine Support Unit. "Anyway, I was just telling your SOCO that I've found something of interest twenty-three yards up the bank. It's a jacket. Possibly owned by the victim. Size and cut matches anyway. Even if it's not his, it could be evidence, don't you think, sir?"

"How did you find it?"

"Hogan did. He's a canine," she says. Or at least, that's what it sounds like.

"What time?"

"Oh ten hundred."

"Do you mud lark around here?" you ask.

"I'm just walking the dog. I work over there. Usually avoid the river during my time off. But this soppy so and so loves the banks. Lots of interesting smells."

At this point, Aksoy has come over, curiously. You explain to him this lady has found something she thinks is evidence.

"Thanks ma'am, but we need to keep this area clear."

She smiles. "Actually, I'm—"

But you hold up your hand to stop her – there's no need.

## Why is this woman's input particularly trustworthy?

Solution on page 202

# FOLLOW THE WEED

The woman leads you to an area that bends away from the river leading under a boardwalk.

"It's over there, I won't come, extra boots will just compromise the scene. Just follow the trails of river weed…"

# Find your way through the maze to the jacket.

It's important not to compromise the scene. Everything should be handled with care to avoid contamination in the lab.

Solution on page 202

# RIPPING YARN

**You find the jacket** under the boardwalk. It's a large black leather duster of uncertain vintage, surprisingly not very damp, despite its location. Normally, you would return to the lab with this before inspecting it, but white marks nearby indicate several torn pieces of paper and, checking the pocket, you find many other matching pieces.

person you

to meet me

our usual

I know

to see b

at 4pm

want

spot.

I'm the last

ut you have

tommorrow,

## Piece the note back together to discover the message.

Your lif

e depends o

joke!

n it.

No

Solution on page 203

# GOOD NEIGHBOURS

**Aksoy takes the body** and the other evidence back to the lab to be processed.

DI Kelvin Kempster, the most experienced pathologist on the FAD team, looks at the body. "Puncture wound right in the back," he says. "I'd say it was a bullet, but there's nothing in there — not even shards. Maybe stabbed with a pipe?"

He agrees with Aksoy about the insects. "Yes, a lot of black soldier flies on this fellow. But there are also grass particles, plant matter, even food waste. Half a tomato in his left armpit. He was either a very messy eater or the body was stored in a bloody compost pit. Based on the lividity, I'd say about a week."

Aksoy nods. "By analyzing the type of grass, food and animal waste, we could work out exactly who he is."

DI Beckhoff enters the room and speaks a couple of words in Aksoy's ear. He looks disappointed.

"His name's Kevin Bunch. His parents reported him missing a week ago."

Aksoy cues up Bunch's file on the computer. "Twenty-two, lives in student accommodation near Goldsmiths University where he's studying art history. To the FAD-mobile!"

Bunch's student accommodation was a shared house. It even had a garage with a beaten-up looking Land Rover parked in front laden with gardening tools. Aksoy leaps through the side gate into the back garden, almost tripping over a row of muddy wellies, before immediately coming back to you with a shrug.

"No compost heap. The space back there's the size of a postage stamp with no flowerbeds or even potted plants."

An elderly gentlemen gives you a wave from the house next door as you ring the doorbell.

He lived with two other Art History students, a History and Anthropology student, and a Sociology postgrad. They're upset but unsurprised that he was found dead on the riverbank. You question three of

them on their ratty sofa while Tianka, the sociology student, brings you a cup of tea. You move some papers to make room for the cup and notice a letter from a Mr Strachan thanking them for helping him "pull up the docks and keep the bushes at bay."

"He was obsessed with larking," says Norman, another Art History student. "I mean, we all did it for a bit, even Tianka…"

"NO, I never did!" Tianka, the Sociology student, insists a little too forcefully. "Anyway. We all mostly gave it up a month ago."

Jillian suddenly chips in, "He was always wandering off, disappearing for days. That's why we didn't report him. Did he drown?"

You keep the method of death to yourself but do mention that he died about a week ago, asking for alibis. None of them can vouch for each other.

Aksoy emerges from the kitchen bearing a small plastic bin with "Food scraps for Mr S's heap" written on it.

"Do you have a compost heap anywhere around here?" he asks.

They look surprised by this but they all nod.

# Where is the compost heap?

Solution on page 203

# THE WRITE STUFF

Seeking to find whoever wrote the note, you collect handwriting samples from the four occupants of the house, to match with the sample.

> I know I'm the last person you want
>
> to see but you have to meet me
>
> at 4pm tommorrow, our usual spot.
>
> Your life depends on it.
>
> No joke!

## Whose handwriting most closely matches that of the note?

**Solution on page 203**

## Tianka Eland

Butter,

Eggs,

Cream Cheese,

Skim Milk,

Carrots

## Wesley Bryant

Can whoever keeps taking my biscuits please buy more tommorrow?

## Jillian Fosdyke

I'm yearning for your hot breath on my neck tomorrow night

## Norman Wingert

Idea:

A novel like Game of Thrones, but instead, all the characters are bandicoots.

# A BOLT FROM THE BLUE

**As Bryant wrote** the note, you suggest interrogating him at the crime scene. Maybe being there will cause him to reveal something.

Strachan's garden is small but well-kept, and Aksoy locates the compost heap with excitement. Strachan is indoors. He's in his nineties, confined to a wheelchair and slightly senile.

Wesley Bryant arrives flanked by two PCs.

"Mr Bryant!" says Aksoy cheerfully. "Show me around?"

"I don't help the others in the garden – too busy. I'm in a medieval re-enactment society."

"Are you a knight? A lancer? Do you use crossbows or a trebuchet?"

"Well, actually..."

You ask Bryant directly why he tried to forge a note from Jillian to Kevin. He chokes.

"It was a joke. They hooked up last year and then fell out... It was a joke!"

A SOCO comes out and reveals that Mr Strachan's nurse put a camera in the garden because he thought vandals were breaking his birdhouse. Cueing up the footage, you see Bunch standing in the garden when he suddenly reacts to some kind of unseen impact and topples forward.

"Hmm, it really does look like he was shot," says Aksoy. "But there was no bullet, or even shrapnel in the wound."

You have a different idea after seeing the footage. You ask Aksoy if he's heard of ice bullets.

"Sure, it's an old chestnut. Make a bullet out of ice, melts in the wound, no evidence. Except the bullet's too brittle and melts in the heat of the explosion from the gun. But something that could propel the ice at speed without an explosion might work."

## How was Kevin Bunch killed?

Solution on page 204

# MUD LARKS

**There's no footage** of the body being removed, as the camera is ironically blocked by a pair of magpies near the birdhouse. Bryant clams up as soon as he realizes he's a suspect, and the weapon is nowhere to be found in their house.

On your way back to the lab, Aksoy gets a message from Beckhoff. "It seems our friend Bunch was, in fact, a petty criminal: he didn't have a mud-larking permit. So anything he found he couldn't claim."

Aksoy and Kempster take another look at the body.

"Look at this… just underneath this finger, a sliver of clay," says Kempster.

Aksoy analyses it and… "There are traces of bird faeces, but the clay is about one-and-a-half thousand years old. Could be from an ancient pot. So he did find treasure? Even a hoard?"

"Great, now we have a weapon and a hoard to find."

"About that…"

Tianka Eland, the Sociology postgrad, was caught trying to sneak onto the crime scene. She works in event management and helped arrange special evenings where the centrepiece was ice sculptures!

You let Bryant see that you've brought Tianka in, who, realizing the "perfect crime" wasn't perfect, now wants to talk.

"She borrowed my crossbow for a 'project'. We've been sleeping together… She had me forge the note too, but I never thought she'd… Oh, God…"

Tianka blames it all on Bryant; says Bunch found the hoard and told them but wanted to confess about his lack of licence. She feared they'd lose the money, and she had big debts, so they murdered him. The only thing she won't confess is the location of the hoard.

"Does she think she can collect it once she's released from prison?"

Solution on page 204

**Where is the hoard?**

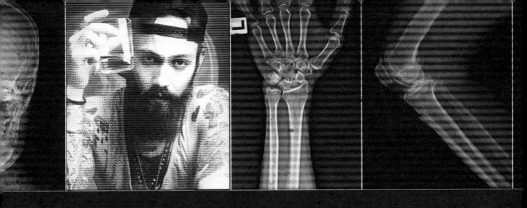

# CSI CHAPTER 4:
# OPERATION **GUINEAFOWL**

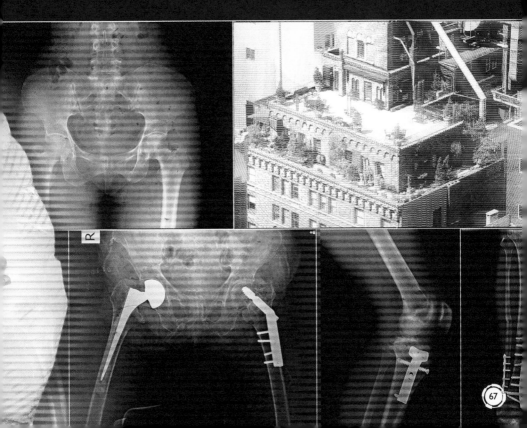

# WE ARE THE CRIME SCENE PRESERVATION SOCIETY

**Jack Vernon is surly** and avoids your cases, preferring to work with other detectives. However, one day, you're surprised to see Vernon approach you in the middle of putting his coat on.

"Right, come with me. Smash-and-grab job, warehouse in Barnet."

The entire building has been cordoned off. The huge double doors at the front of the building are wrenched off their hinges. Shattered brickwork litters the ground. Inside, it's chaotic: boxes scattered around, doors kicked through, and the floor covered in litter. You can see that the SOCOs have followed the guidelines for preserving a crime scene:

- Set up a blockade.
- Mark off the perimeter with police tape.
- Scene-of-Crime Officers may not eat, drink, smoke or take breaks in or near the scene.
- Evidence must only be handled by police wearing protective gloves.

The warehouse's owner is Mr Panjit. He seems almost excited by the events. "No one was here, oh no! The watchman had gone out to buy some cigarettes. He's been harshly reprimanded, of course. But what a lucky break for him, otherwise perhaps he'd have been harmed."

Vernon doesn't even bother talking to him and wanders off. You wonder if Mr Panjit is either very naive or very good at lying.

"I am a great respecter of the police," continues Mr Panjit, "so I have made sure to keep the crime scene perfect! Sticky tape everywhere so no one could get in, no smoking or eating here… In fact, I threw away any food that I found. And I gathered pieces of the broken wall for evidence; I put them in plastic bags!"

He grins.

## Has Mr Panjit done a good job of preserving the crime scene?

Solution on page 204

# TOTAL RUBBISH

"**Of course**, the other reason I removed the food is it was meat. We do not eat meat – our religion forbids it."

You ask Mr Panjit what was stolen. You already know what has been claimed, but it's important to hear it from his perspective.

"My entire stock of high-fashion clothing! Cashmere sweaters, designer jeans, T-shirts imported from France and Italy. These will be very well-dressed robbers, I think."

Vernon beckons you over, shooting Mr Panjit a dirty look. He points at a mark on one of the internal doors that has been removed.

"See this? Diamond-tipped bandsaw. That's an SWIX gang trademark. Mr Smiley over there has just been robbed by the biggest organized-crime gang in London."

SWIX is the organization that your superiors suspect may have the mole in the department. Several of the cases that were compromised had to do with them.

Vernon rubs his face wearily.

"Very professional job, as usual. I don't think we'll find them. To be honest, Panjit's probably part of a rival gang – they always are. Let them all wreck each other, I say."

You ask him about all the litter on the floor, looking at cardboard boxes and sandwich wrappers, marked with the words "Barbecue Bob's".

"Oh yeah. This is their usual trick, all right. Scatter a bunch of rubbish on the floor – complicates the forensic profile incredibly – make us bag and tag a hundred pieces of crap: absolutely charming. But they're not as clever as they think."

He picks up a packet. "There's an easy way to tell what belongs here and what doesn't."

**Solution on page 204**

## How can you tell what has been emptied in the warehouse from the litter?

# YOU MIST

**You get one** of the police officers to escort Mr Panjit away and then draw Jack Vernon's attention to something. It's a bullet hole in the wall!

He rolls his eyes, then touches it carefully. "Yeah, this is fresh. Let's check for more."

In all, you find four different bullet holes in the warehouse.

"See, what did I tell you? Designer clothes, my arse. It was the bloody Wild Wild West in here last night."

He turns to a nearby SOCO. "Go to the van. Get the bloody high-def lasers and tripods. And the mist machine."

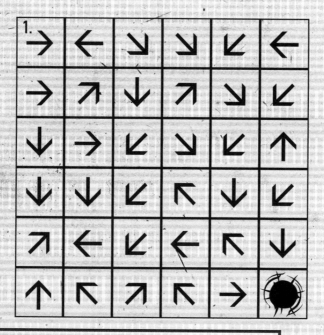

**To plot the trajectory of the bullets, move from top left to the hole on the bottom right. You need not stop on every square. The arrows in each square show which direction you must move in.**

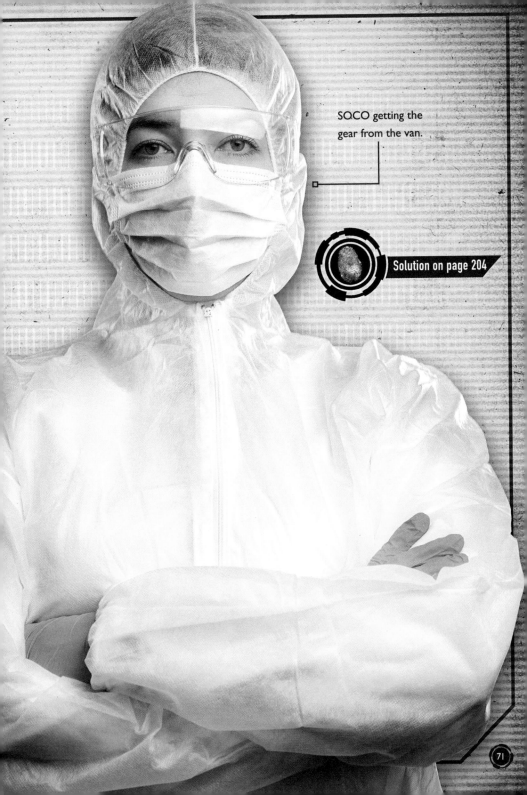

SOCO getting the
gear from the van.

Solution on page 204

# USING YOUR LOAF

**Mr Panjit is horrified** to hear that there may have been gunfire in his warehouse. "Oh my goodness, really? Terrible."

The supposed night-watchman also knows nothing and is as "shocked" as Mr Panjit.

No shell casings are found and the gun residue extracted from the bullet holes is generic. DI Vernon seems uncaring. While clearing up, you find something that doesn't match: a piece of bread in a plain wrapper that doesn't resemble the other litter. You take it back to the lab with everything else. Everyone gathers as you bring in the boxes.

"Not the SW1X again," says Aksoy, shaking his head. Beckhoff raises an eyebrow and goes back to her office, while Kempster comes over and starts helping you unload.

"I can help with this. Is there anything in particular you want to fast-track?"

You take the crust to Vernon's lab and put it under the microscope. Vernon gives you a baleful look.

"What are you thinking? That it's full of cocaine?"

Actually, you're trying to see if there's anything distinctive about the bread that could help you narrow it down to a location: wheat type, unusual seeds, the method of baking… But you're far from a baking expert, so you bring one in. A few emails and, in half an hour, you're shaking hands with Amy Grigoletti, author of *The Forensic Baker*.

"What makes you forensic? Do you give evidence about bread in court?" comments Vernon snarkily, before wandering off.

"The title was the publisher's idea," she says apologetically. "I didn't even know what forensic meant. They just wanted it to sound scientific. But I'm glad to help."

You show her the bread in question and she looks at your slides, and then breaks the piece apart, rubbing it between her fingers, smelling, then tasting.

"It's a pumpernickel/bloomer hybrid. There are variations on this available all around London, I'm afraid, but the poppy seeds are distinctive, and it's quite salty. There's something about the flavour… It's olive oil!"

On a hunch, you ask her if she can think of any places in Knightsbridge that might sell this.

"Let's have a look online," she suggests.

"It should be the kind of place criminals would be happy to visit," Vernon adds.

After some minutes of searching, she's found five possibilities, all artisanal bakeries.

Cocaine laced?

"There's Harriet's Kitchen. They've got a good selection. Very busy place all the time; big queues. The Poppy House. Ever since that was endorsed by that actor from Met Squad, ALL the police hang out in there. Er, no offence. Atmos. That's this super-trendy place. They won't let you have takeaway. If they see you try to leave with the bread, they'll slap it out of your hand! Casa del Olivio. They opened a few months ago – well reviewed. And then Blondini's. They're vegan. If you wear leather shoes in there, they spit in your kombucha. Have I been any help?"

**HARRIET'S KITCHEN**

**THE POPPY HOUSE**

**CASA DEL OLIVIO**

**ATMOS**

**BLONDINI'S**

## Which café did the bread come from?

Solution on page 205

# THIS SUCKS

**You tell Vernon** you need to head to the café.

"Great, get me an espresso," he says.

You give him a look and he grumpily gets up from his chair and picks up a small case next to him. "At least I get to try out my new toy, I suppose."

Casa del Olivio is a small café that was once someone's front room, and it's deep in the dodgier end of Knightsbridge. It has handwritten recipe boards, a whimsical tip jar made from a hollowed-out brick, and a series of carefully mismatched chairs and tables. When you enter, a healthy-looking lady gives you a big smile.

"What would you like?"

You show her your warrant card and ask her name. She's the café owner, Isabella López. You ask her about her customers over the last day or so. Were there any suspicious looking groups of men?

"How do you define suspicious?" she asks playfully. But then she admits there was a group of four men in the café the night before, around 8 p.m., talking very closely, but tipping very generously.

"So generously you won't give us a description?"

"I'm not good at that. They were all bald, medium height, black jackets. They sat at that table, but all their plates and cups have been washed, I'm afraid."

Vernon is brandishing a tiny vacuum cleaner behind you, looking disappointed. It's an M-Vac: a modern forensic tool that allows you to collect DNA off normally non-viable surfaces, such as porous ones, that make extraction difficult or impossible.

Isabella Lopez,
proprietor

## Where should Vernon use his M-Vac?

Solution on page 205

# SKIN DEEP

**Back at the lab,** you run the DNA profiles of several different samples you get off the tip jar and, after eliminating the owner, her workers and a few regular customers, you identify a likely suspect: Fyodor Bykov, long suspected of gang activity but none of it proven.

Bykov's only registered address is a lock-up in Pimlico, so you travel there quickly, accompanied by Vernon, who is pretending not to care.

At the lock-up, a local kid offers information in exchange for a look at the M-Vac. "Yeah, I saw Mr Biker. He was here this morning but he left in his car with some other bloke."

You ask for a description and get the same "short hair, black jacket, etc." account you got from Isabella, but then the boy smiles. "He had a tattoo. Reckon you're clever? Here's a riddle: 'I have two rings, I move by request; if the mixture is not right, I just sit at rest.'" He wanders off chuckling.

## Which tattoo is indicated by the riddle the boy just recited?

**Solution on page 205**

# CLOSED CIRCUIT

**You pull the details** on Bykov's car, wondering if it could have been the one used in the robbery. Not a lot of room for "luxury goods" in the boot but, if they were stealing something else, it's possible. Usually, a gang would use a stolen car for something like this, which makes you uncertain.

You return to the lab to find that DI Beckhoff has pulled all of the CCTV from the surrounding area. "Before this, you'd have been wading through vehicle registrations for months, but now, there's a chance. Don't waste it," she says, eyeing an uncaring Vernon.

You look at the footage and find a few possibilities. Prove how perceptive you are by analysing the two stills below.

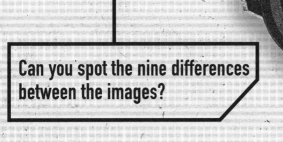

Can you spot the nine differences between the images?

Solution on page 205

# CODE RED

**DI Vernon then gets another message.** "Well, that's horribly inevitable," he says. "Let's go to the Docklands."

When you arrive, Bykov's car has already been removed from where it was dumped in the water. Inside is a decapitated, limbless corpse that you would bet is the man himself.

You search the body and all you find is an old library copy of *Farewell to Arms.* Classy.

"I bet it's overdue and all," says DI Vernon. "I doubt any of them have a library card, though."

But something suddenly catches his eye. "Hang on… there's an indentation on the cover."

On close examination, it looks like someone wrote a note using the book as support, and it's visible. You reconstruct the note, only to find it's some kind of cipher.

"A message. But about what?"

*Farewell to Arms,*
  a library book.

MSTOE EKQED EBNCD TOLAW OJWER

NKCDP RWQLC OLLWS OLLWS FPWYT

OAWCC FLMEKR CSKDD RPCKD OTSDF

SKDSC SMCOT KLKDF EVVCN YUIOP

What does the message say?

Solution on page 206

# FLIGHT OF FANCY

**After a quick search**, you find a pub in Chinatown called The Crossed Keys. On arrival, the landlord, Simon Dupree, is as friendly and baffled as Mr Panjit.

"Never had any impropriety," he says. "Sometimes the children in the house that backs onto our garden are a bit noisy, losing balls and kites and stuff, but kids will be kids!"

He denies ever having seen Bykov in the pub, but he'd probably deny knowing the Queen to save his own skin.

However, when you suggest that you might need to turn the pub into a crime scene, he suddenly remembers that Bykov had visited and gone up to the roof, where there's a smaller garden, but he doesn't remember any more because it was the end of his shift and he was feeling ill.

You go up to the roof but don't immediately find anything interesting, save bits of broken glass. A glimmer catches your eye and, crouching down, you find a razorblade. Then, behind a chimney pot, you spot a bright-orange ribbon, made of some kind of silken fabric. But nothing else. Looking closer at the glass, you think you can see a speck of blood, but that's all.

You take out a pocket bottle of luminol and spray it on the razor, which, once you cup your hand around it, glows distinctively. Blood. But maybe someone cut themself shaving… on the roof.

Vernon starts staring at something opposite. He's still trying to come across as cynical, but you can tell he is caught up in the chase.

Suddenly, Vernon dashes down the stairs and out of the pub and you follow him as he runs into a small office building a few houses away. He flashes his warrant card and you both enter the lift and go up to the fourth floor, where he dashes over to a shocked-looking woman sitting at her desk and yells, "DOES THAT WEBCAM WORK?"

On accessing the webcam footage, you can now see why Vernon was so driven. The cam was inadvertently pointed directly at the pub and, therefore, acts as an unintentional witness of everything.

The woman, named Kirsty McColl ("I'm not the singer! I mean, obviously, she's dead."), tries to tell Vernon that she wasn't using the camera at the time you are interested in, and then is horrified when he accesses her laptop archives and shows that the camera is, in fact, permanently on. After scrolling past several hours of footage, he finds the time in question, and there is Bykov, small and blurry but distinctive, waiting to meet someone. There's a sudden blur of activity; some kind of diamond shape moving across the screen with a flick of orange...

It's a kite!

"It doesn't make any sense," says Vernon, rewinding and replaying the clip. "A kite? A KITE? How does that kill him?"

You know.

## Who or what killed Bykov?

Rooftop footage of The Crossed Keys public house.

Solution on page 206

# PHONE CARRIER

**After securing the roof,** you move with your SOCO team to the garden that abuts the pub.

These people are ambitious and ruthless, but also sloppy. In the garden, you find a burner mobile. It's cracked so they probably dropped it as they ran but, if you get it back to the lab, it shouldn't be difficult to extract any information it might contain.

Bykov is a dead end, at least in terms of associations, as most of the people you know of him spending time with are either dead, in jail, or nowhere near this level. So this phone is your best chance of a break in the case, to get a real understanding of SW1X.

The next morning, you exit the lift to find Vernon extremely angry, talking to a group of SOCOs roaming around his lab. He rounds on you, baring his teeth. "Was it you? You come into the department, clean boots, "perfect" record – it's all a bit too convenient!"

He then gathers himself. "It's gone. The phone has gone. I have no idea how."

Apparently, he had been bone-tired, so he secured all the evidence, switched off the lights and swiped out with his card. Then, when he returned this morning, the phone was no longer there.

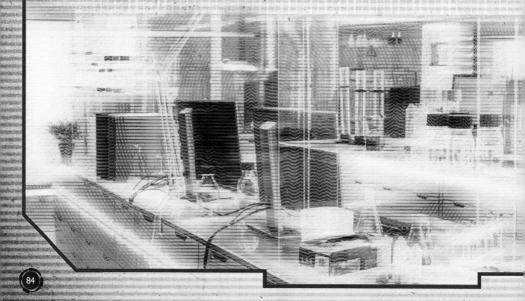

"Anything on the security cameras?"

Vernon swallowed. "I... disconnected them months ago. I hate being watched. I figured with the card keys and the round-the-clock security we have here, they weren't necessary. Yes, I know, I'm probably going to be in the crap for this. But we have to figure out how it was done!"

He pulls a laptop over. "I thought inside job – I don't trust anyone here. But I've looked at the security logs and no one has used a card key since I left last night. You could fiddle with the logs but there's a lot of tricks and traps in here to prevent that. Beckhoff put them in – it's her expertise."

You look around the lab. To the naked eye, nothing seems different. No visible footprints. His lab is spotless, everything carefully cleaned and maintained – his own little sealed kingdom.

"The only other thing that's changed is that this thermos I left on the desk has fallen over. And these printed-out test results scattered on the floor. It's not great evidence."

You look at the test results but they are unrelated to the case, and the thermos just had tea in it.

One of the SOCOs points to an open-air vent on the wall.

"Wow, you've solved it. It was a one-foot tall ninja with rubber bones!" says Vernon scathingly. "That does make me wonder, though: could they have come through the ceiling somehow?"

You inspect the panels and find no sign of disturbance. You look at one of the walls and notice a series of small horizontal scrapes. Crouching down, you see the same series of horizontal scrapes all along the counter just above the floor, which then rises toward where the phone is. They look like they were made by a series of tiny spinning blades. Following this, you notice a dent in one of the doorframes, shaped almost like a big frisbee.

You tell Vernon you think you know what happened.

# What happened to the phone?

Solution on page 206

PA Upright

DECEASED

## JACK VERNON IS DEAD

You're writing an email to your superiors detailing your current suspicions when you get the call. Jack Vernon has died. He had been at a rehearsal for his amateur orchestra (for which he played the tuba), when he suddenly grabbed his throat and keeled over.

Even if his death had seemed to be of natural causes, the timing of it is hugely suspicious. He was investigating SW1X, and the theft of the evidence had enraged him – or so it seemed.

It seems to you that there are only two possibilities: Either Vernon was working for SW1X and they were clearing house...

Or, more likely, the infiltrator within the department now has blood on their hands. Whatever happens, you resolve at this moment: *You will find them and bring them to justice.*

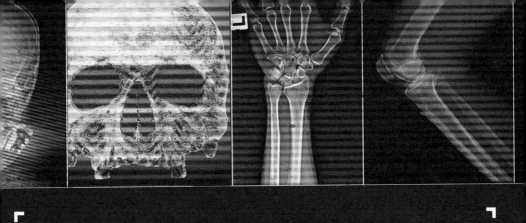

# CSI CHAPTER 5:
# THE DEVIL'S INTERVAL

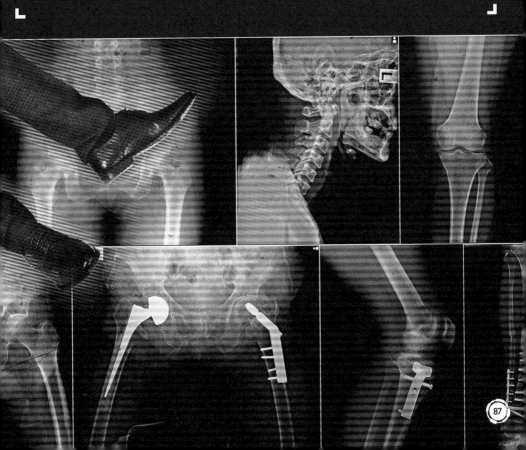

# BEGINNING OF AN END

**The department is in shock** but resolves to carry on as best as they can. Although Vernon was very prickly, he was still quite well respected. Aksoy offers team members support with advice mostly gleaned from mid-nineties TV shows, Beckhoff pretends not to care but you're sure you saw tears in her eyes, and Kempster – possibly Vernon's closest friend in the department – is determined to solve the case.

You start at the scene of Vernon's death, Baxter's Music Hall: a music venue that rents out its spaces to amateur musicians. The scene is already secured.

"Not taking any chances with this. There's no way Jack's death was natural. He deserves our very best."

The body has already been removed and the chairs are scattered from where the brass band leaped up when Vernon keeled over.

"Apparently, the trombone player attempted CPR, but it was fruitless," Kempster says, dramatically kneeling down next to the spot where Vernon collapsed.

You begin looking around nearby and notice something: there's a space in the dust by the door, as if something was once there. The actual shape of it is difficult to discern, however.

Reveal the hidden image by shading in the number of squares indicated in each row and column. The numbers show how many squares must be shaded in a row, and more than one number means there must be a space of at least one square between rows of shaded cells.

| | 3 | 5 | 2 2 | 2 2 | 2 2 4 | 8 2 | 4 2 | 2 2 2 | 5 7 | 8 2 | 4 2 2 | 2 2 2 | 2 2 2 | 2 2 2 | 4 2 2 | 5 2 2 | 7 2 2 | 9 2 2 | 2 2 | 5 | 3 |
|---|---|---|---|---|---|---|---|---|---|---|---|---|---|---|---|---|---|---|---|---|---|
| 1 | | | | | | | | | | | | | | | | | | | | | |
| 2 | | | | | | | | | | | | | | | | | | | | | |
| 1,1,1,3 | | | | | | | | | | | | | | | | | | | | | |
| 1,1,1,4 | | | | | | | | | | | | | | | | | | | | | |
| 16 | | | | | | | | | | | | | | | | | | | | | |
| 17 | | | | | | | | | | | | | | | | | | | | | |
| 2,1,1,4 | | | | | | | | | | | | | | | | | | | | | |
| 2,1,1,2 | | | | | | | | | | | | | | | | | | | | | |
| 2,1,1,1 | | | | | | | | | | | | | | | | | | | | | |
| 2,1,1 | | | | | | | | | | | | | | | | | | | | | |
| 17 | | | | | | | | | | | | | | | | | | | | | |
| 17 | | | | | | | | | | | | | | | | | | | | | |
| 1,2 | | | | | | | | | | | | | | | | | | | | | |
| 1,2 | | | | | | | | | | | | | | | | | | | | | |
| 1,1,3 | | | | | | | | | | | | | | | | | | | | | |
| 2,13 | | | | | | | | | | | | | | | | | | | | | |
| 2,11 | | | | | | | | | | | | | | | | | | | | | |
| 1 | | | | | | | | | | | | | | | | | | | | | |
| | | | | | | | | | | | | | | | | | | | | | |
| | | | | | | | | | | | | | | | | | | | | | |
| | | | | | | | | | | | | | | | | | | | | | |

Solution on page 206

# DOUBLE TROUBLE

**Back at the lab**, you suspect Kempster may be getting a little too overzealous when he models the entire rehearsal room on his computer. You leave him to it, but an hour later, he comes to you looking frantic.

"Have you seen anyone using my terminal?" he asks. "Someone's altered my model of the rehearsal room; interfered with it. See?"

# Can you spot the five differences between the unaltered and altered rehearsal room simulation?

Solution on page 207

# KILLER INSTINCT

**Ultimately**, you have to analyse Jack Vernon's body. Although it's not your first time seeing a dead colleague on the slab, it never loses the visceral impact. You can see that Kempster is affected as well, but he stays professional.

The coroner begins his report. "The… body shows no outward signs of physical trauma; expression is strangely serene. Lips, eyes, teeth seem normal. But the skin is a dark-maroon colour, except in some patches."

He makes the incision.

"Internally, lungs have expanded at the bottom. Pulmonary edema is apparent. Massive strain on heart evident. No signs of haemorrhaging. I… think he was poisoned."

Kempster thinks about this for a moment. "Hmm, there are a few possibilities. Arsenic in high enough doses kills you gradually: all your organs eventually fail, you haemorrhage… usually with burns or redness around the lips. Ricin is popular in assassinations – deadly in very small doses. Blood vomiting, organ failure again. Cyanide blocks your ability to use oxygen – very fast acting. You get dizzy and breathe rapidly, fluid in the lungs, your skin turns cherry red then goes darker red… then cardiac arrest. And strychnine: now that's nasty. Your muscles start spasming again and again in increased intensity, with a rictus grin, until the convulsions destroy all your neural pathways and exhaust you to death!"

He gives you a guilty look. You observe that it's not abnormal for a crime-scene investigator to have an interest in poisons.

The coroner coughs awkwardly and continues: "Yes, well… we'll test his blood and cells, but I think we both know which poison was probably used here, don't we?"

## Which poison was used: arsenic, ricin, cyanide or strychnine?

Solution on page 207

# SO IT BEGINS

Study these objects carefully for one minute. Memorise them as best you can.

**Now turn over.**

# Without looking back, can you work out which item is missing?

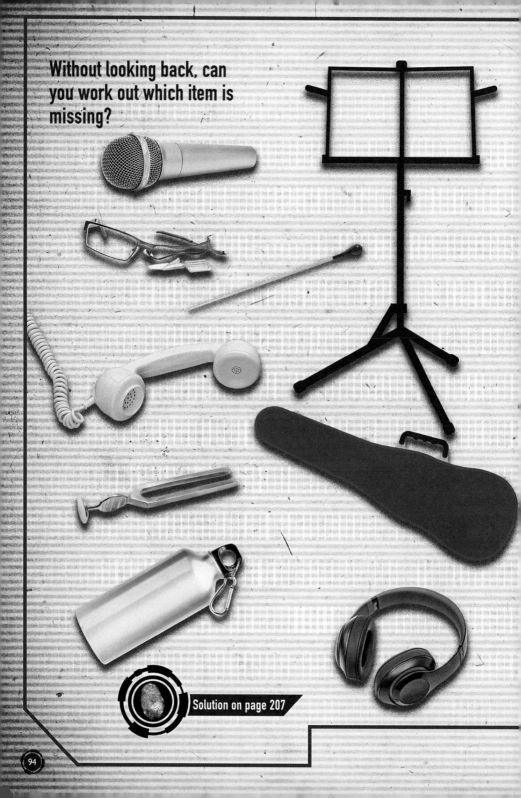

Solution on page 207

# A DOG'S LIFE

**Kempster analyzes** the hair on Vernon's head under a microscope. He looks up with surprise. "It seems Jack Vernon… had fleas!"

You look at the hair and observe, with your entomological knowledge, that they are, in fact, dog fleas.

"This suggests he came into close contact with a dog owner shortly before death because, as you can see, they have died from drinking his blood. Out of his bandmates, who owned a dog?" you ask.

By looking online at their social-media pages, you identify five dogs owned by the amateur musicians.

## From the pictures, can you work out which dog the fleas came from?

Solution on page 207

# HIS MASTER'S VOICE

**Kempster wants to return** to the crime scene to see if you can find the phone and microphone, but when you arrive, you find a small contingent of the musicians. They're asking when they can get back in to collect their instruments.

"Who here is Phil Deal?" asks Kempster.

A short man wearing a scarf puts his hand up. "That's me," he says in a rather husky voice, letting out a cloud of bad breath you can smell from where you are.

"You own a Jack Russell named Trinket, right?" quizzes Kempster. "We need to chat."

You sit with Deal, who plays the lead trumpet in the band. He admits that he took the mobile phone but refuses to say why, feeling his throat while his eyes nervously look toward the group of musicians still nearby. He avoids eye contact and toys with a plastic wristband that has his name and date of birth on it.

"I think I already know why you took it," says Kempster, and Deal looks up, surprised.

Kempster continues: "I don't mean to be blunt but do you have a throat problem? With an operation coming up?"

Deal nods reluctantly.

"It's a quinsy; pus in an abscess. I don't want to lose my lead-trumpeter position! My flow's already not what it was. The recording on the phone might be my last performance. I thought if it went into your evidence, it might get deleted."

Deal hands the phone over and slinks off.

## How did Kempster work out that Deal had a throat problem?

Solution on page 207

# SMILEY FACE

**Back at the lab,** you access the phone but, for some reason, its owner has changed all the song titles to emojis, making it difficult to find the relevant file.

Can you decode the famous pop songs represented by these emojis?

Solution on page 208

# THE ART OF NOISE

**You help DI Beckhoff** with some tissue analysis, leaving Kempster to analyze the audio. When you return to his lab, Kempster tells you that, unfortunately, it doesn't really give any clues to the murder, being a fairly standard recording of an amateur band. You listen yourself and have to agree that there's nothing notably odd, although you do suggest it might be worth listening to the occasionally spoken words you can hear in the background.

"Talk to Aksoy – he does audio analysis," Kempster suggests.

Aksoy is more than happy to import the sound file into some audio software he has and separate it out into individual tracks. But, as he does so, he notes, "I have some forensic audio experience and I think this has been messed with. I think one of the tracks on here is a fake."

## Which audio track is fake?

## Lead Trumpet

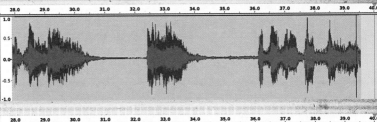

## French horn

A: French horn bumps elbow into second tuba and says, 'Oh, excuse me.'

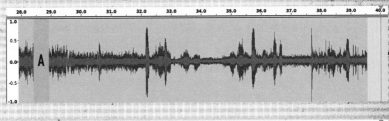

## Second Trumpet

A: Second trumpet humming along with trombone for some reason.

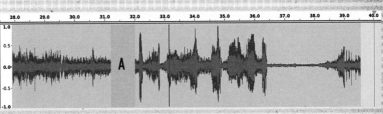

## Trombone

A: Trombone asks flute to stop eating crisps.

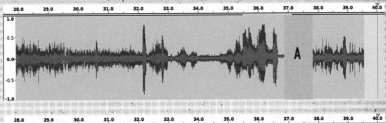

## Flute

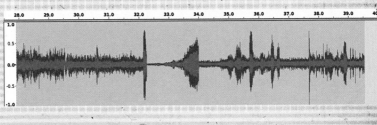

## Second Tuba

Second tuba, AKA DI Vernon, dies.

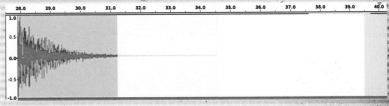

Solution on page 208

# BREAKING GLASS

**You speak to the band's** ostensible leader, Charlie Wolowicz, about who was playing the flute. "Oh yeah, he was this new bloke. Turned up for the wrong session but he was such a nice fella we decided to let him sit in for a laugh." He can't seem to remember his name but promises to ask the others.

Returning to the crime scene to collect fingerprints, you find a series of glass shards near where the flautist was but, after Vernon's death, there was a panic and a number of objects were damaged. You're not sure which particular breakage the shards come from.

Solution on page 208

Which of these breakages do the shards come from?

A

B

C

# BOTTLE ROCKET

**Kempster gets a call** from Beckhoff. She's re-autopsied the body and found something lodged in Vernon's throat: a blow-dart!

"Amazing. The flute itself was the weapon. It blew the dart right into Jack's mouth when he was taking a breath. Why did they kill him like this?"

You point out that you confiscated all the instruments but that there was no flute.

"Yes, he's hidden or disposed of it."

He crouches by the broken window. "Burn marks, and little bits of burned plastic. In all the ruckus, some of the musicians said they heard a fizzing sound like a firework. What if he put the flute in something like a bottle rocket?"

Further analysis of the scene indicates that this theory is correct. The window is on the third floor, nine metres off the ground, and the scorch marks indicate that the rocket was fired almost exactly horizontally.

Back at the lab, you experiment with bottle rockets. With a flute inside, the average rocket travels at 20 metres per second – you don't find any traces of fuel at the scene so you are confident that it can't have gone much faster.

## How far from the window should you search for the flute? You can assume air resistance is negligible, gravity is 10m/s² and you will need the equation $d = 0.5 \times a \times t^2$.

Solution on page 208

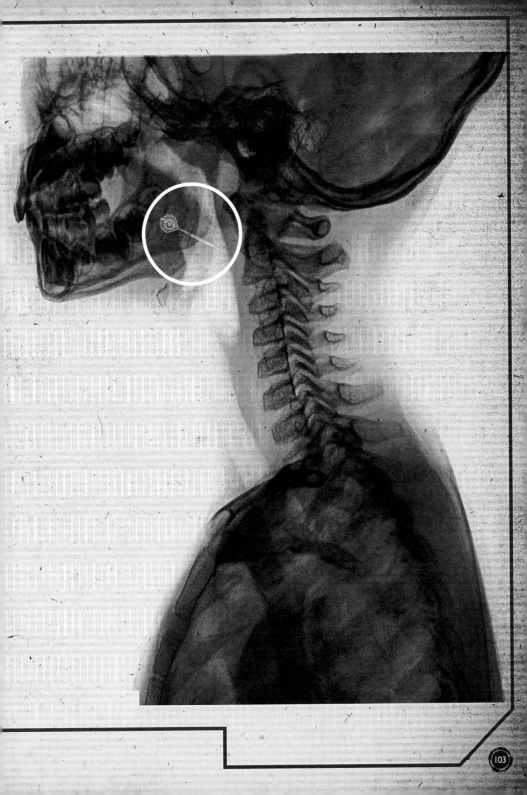

PA Upright

104

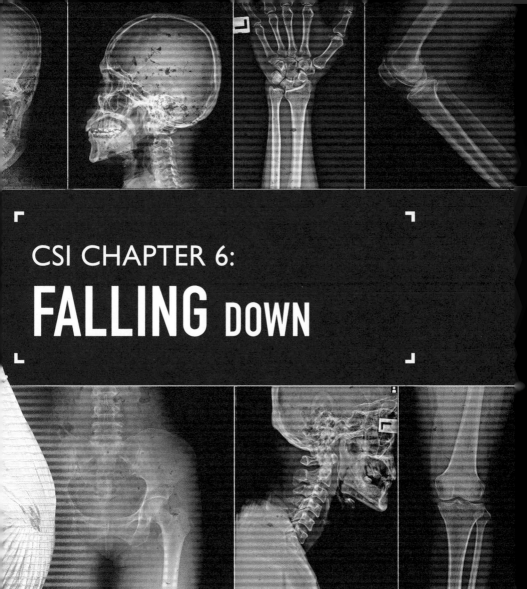

# CSI CHAPTER 6:
# FALLING DOWN

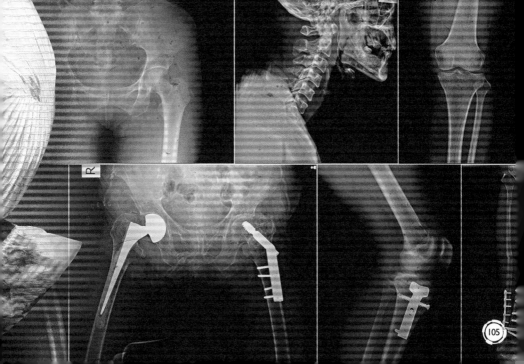

# PUZZLE 51 THAT'S TORN IT

**Despite your calculation,** you don't find the murder weapon; only useless trace evidence. The mysterious flautist has disappeared. Kempster is frustrated and angry.

This is interrupted by an urgent new case: a balcony has collapsed at The Bridge, a legendary London nightclub, resulting in the death of three people.

The nightclub was originally an old music hall in the 1920s and still maintains some of its original features, like the two giant copper statues of Greek Muses, now looking more like the Statue of Liberty from verdigris discolouration.

Inside it's alternately cramped and expansive, hasty repairs with rusty nails and wooden boards in some places and modern renovations in others. The balcony lies in the centre of the main dancefloor, shattered into huge chunks of masonry.

Before you go in you put on your protective suits as usual.

"I actually used to come here in the eighties," says Kempster thoughtfully. "I looked so ridiculous. It's actually a lot less run down now."

You move forward to the collapsed balcony. Among the stone rubble and the spikily twisted-up antique copper railings of the balcony is a mess of broken champagne bottles mixing with smashed chairs and tables, and, of course, the bodies. Furthermore, the balcony had landed on a bank of TV screens, smashing them to bits.

Kempster suddenly stops. "My suit is torn, see?" he says, showing you a big hole in his side with a strange green stain around it. "I'll go change it," he says. "Can't risk cross-contamination."

You're not sure, but you think you know where it got torn, and tell him to be more careful next time.

## Where did it get torn?

Solution on page 209

# BLAME GAME

**Once Kempster has** changed, you start analyzing the scene, which is difficult because of the sheer quantity of wreckage and evidence.

"The balcony is an antique obviously, but it's been repeatedly repaired and reinforced over decades, kept up to health-and-safety code," says Kempster, referring to files on his phone. "So the question is, did the last people do a shoddy job? Or was there another factor?"

Neither you nor Kempster are experts in balcony construction. Once you've gathered your evidence, you can consult one. But you have an understanding of elementary construction, and you notice that the steel brackets that provided the balcony's main support structures have enormous, strangely organic holes in them, almost like something has eaten through them. There is also a strong acrid smell coming from them. The holes have crumbly edges. In fact, in places, the steel has tracks all the way down it, like drips from some kind of liquid.

You find similar marks on carpet and exposed floorboards among the rubble. Everywhere in the crime scene is the accompanying pungent, acrid smell.

Strangely, there are no marks on any of the plastic components of the balcony's support. Mentally reconstructing the brackets, you can see the damage starts roughly at the top, where the people would be standing, and travels all the way down.

Kempster is observing the same on the other side. "So the possibilities for the collapse, as I see them, are normal wear-and-tear, poor construction, or some kind of corrosive agent. I'm leaning towards corrosive. What do you think? Any ideas what it could have been?"

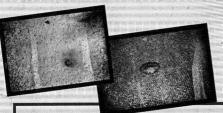

## Can you think of an agent that could have caused the damage?

Solution on page 209

# PUZZLING EVIDENCE

"**Any device used to do** something like that would probably be dangerous. The person who used it would want to get rid of it quickly."

You both have the same thought and make your way to the alley at the back of the club, where the bins are kept.

**A**

**B**

**C**

**D**

**E**

One of these bins has vital
evidence in it. Which one?

Solution on page 209

# PEOPLE TAKE PICTURES

**Kempster grabs a SOCO.** "We need this sealed off immediately. It's a dangerous hazard."

Talking to one of the security guards, you find out that a man was seen throwing something into that particular bin, but after the collapse he'd forgotten about it. He gives you a description and you arrange for a facial composite to be made of the suspect.

"Well, there should be an easy way of finding this man," says Kempster. "Thank goodness for social media." Using the composite you are easily able to find a photo of him from earlier in the night. Would you have been able to help the police as much as the security guard?

Look at this picture for 1 minute and turn over.

Solution on page 209

Can you create a composite
of the culprit from memory?

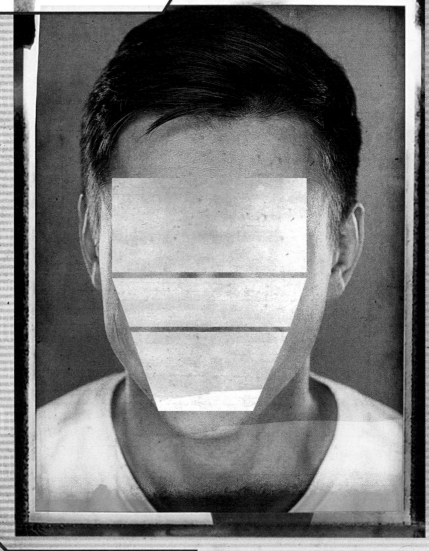

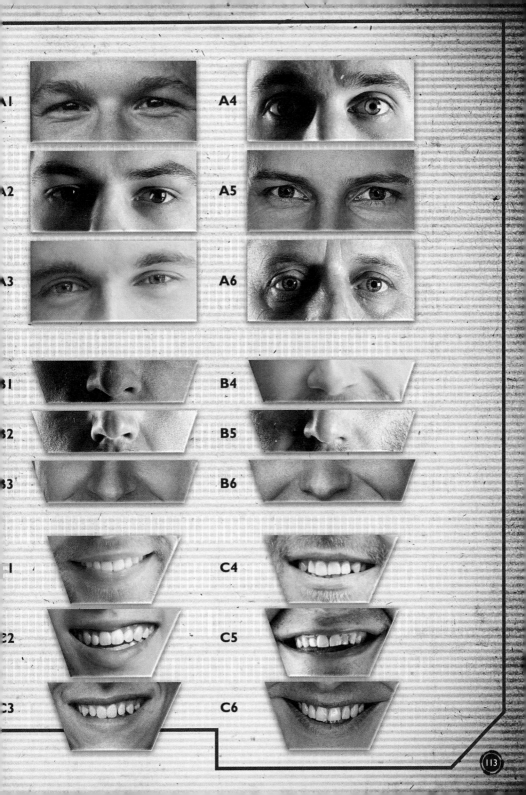

A1  A4

A2  A5

A3  A6

B1  B4

B2  B5

B3  B6

C1  C4

C2  C5

C3  C6

113

# KISS

**Even with the photo,** you can't get a name for the person disposing of what you find to be a plastic sealant applicator, adapted to discharge hydrofluoric acid. However, there's an interesting clue in the picture: a kiss mark on one cheek.

"Oh yeah, that was a promotion we had," says the manager. "Triang Make-up were launching six new lipsticks, so they had six ladies, each wearing one, going around kissing people."

Thinking someone at Triang may be able to help, you contact the company to find out who was wearing the colour from the photo, but they are deeply unhelpful. All they do is send you a list of the lipsticks with their colours and names – and they all arrive as separate files.

Alto 289     Mar 25, 1999 18:4

Royal Rumble - Vanessa

London Bus - Rachel

Think - Amaya

LA Noir - Vicky

Glistering - Jacky

Ecowarrior - Tahani

750

Solution on page 210

0 5 0 11:00 Y:00 +2.20

# FALSE POSITIVES, FALSE NEGATIVES

**You return to the lab** with Kempster, with the now carefully isolated acid sprayer. There is still a lot of evidence at the crime scene but you need to act quickly if you want to catch the suspect.

Looking at its construction, Kempster says it's clearly the work of a single amateur.

You disagree when you analyze it yourself, feeling it would have to have been professionally made to ensure the acid wouldn't leak before use, and to maximize its ability to spray at the right time onto the balcony.

"Well… if we test the acid, we can probably get an idea as to whether it's an industrial type, or if it's been made from a mixture or extracted from somewhere."

Kempster very carefully puts a sample of the acid in the Gas Chromatograph-Mass Spectrometer and then, looking at the computer screen, does a double take.

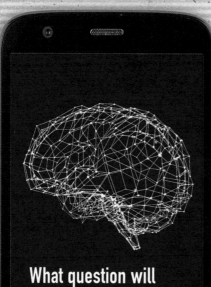

"It's spat out two different results. One says the acid is pure, industrial grade; the other says it's adulterated. I think there's a glitch in… never mind."

You tell him to go on.

"Designing AIs – artificial intelligences – is a hobby of mine. I installed one in the GC-MS, but it's become wilful. I think it's split into two. One AI always gives true results and the other false. Without knowing which is which, we won't be able to get the right result. We need to use someone else's equipment."

You ask if the AIs will respond to questions, and when Kempster says they will, you know exactly what question to ask one of them.

## What question will allow you to work out which AI always tells the truth and which always lies?

Solution on page 210

# NAME AND NUMBER

**You get a call:** Amaya, the pink-lipstick girl, has identified the man as a regular club-goer named Derek Rankin. The police have apprehended him but he's claimed total ignorance of any of the night's events.

Considering both the design of the acid shooter and his actions, you suspect that he wasn't acting alone and may, in fact, have been hired to do this.

Before talking to Rankin, you decide to pull all the information from his phone. It shows the calls he's received, but everyone on there has a weird nickname obscuring their identity.

Derek Rankin, wilfully ignorant.

1. **Pouty Pants**
2. **Unibrow**
3. **Piglet**
4. **Wookie**
5. **Inspector Hound**

A     B     C     D     E

## Can you match the phone nicknames to the photos of his known associates?

Solution on page 210

# SUBTEXTS

The individual he calls "Unibrow" is a known gangland figure and drug dealer, with big connections. You look at the texts they have exchanged, but they appear to be in code.

**9G**

1. 7 9 3 13 5 3 18 - 7 10 22 - 22 7 9 - 23 17 1 - 6 11 6

2. 21 23 17 20 7 9 16 3 6 - 14 14 7 25 - 21 22 11 - 21 11 10 22 - 20 17 8 - 3 20 22 26 7 - 22 7 9 - 6 14 23 17 10 21 - 11 - 22 23 4 - 10 3 7 1

3. 7 25 17 - 23 17 1 - 20 7 4 15 7 15 7 20 - 22 11 - 7 24 3 7 14 - 20 17 - 22 11 - 7 13 3 22

4. 10 9 23 17 10 22 - 7 11 6 - 7 14 18 17 7 18 - 20 7 10 22 17 - 22 16 17 25

5. 7 16 17 6 - 22 11 - 22 7 9 - 22 3 10 22 - 7 13 11 14 - 7 22 11 10 21 - 1 3 21 - 22 16 17 6

## Can you decipher the messages?

Unibrow, a notorious gangland figure.

Solution on page 210

119

# WHO ARE YOU?

The messages suggest the balcony was tampered with in order to kill one particular person. Back at headquarters, you have the three bodies and a number of personal items.

**Bob Dobalina**

**Mary Pynchon**

**Matthias Athanasio**

A

B

C

D

E

REPUBLICA DE NICARAGUA
DIRECCION GENERAL DE MIGRACION Y EXTRANJERIA
CEDULA DE RESIDENCIA

F

IBIZA
ALL ISLANDS IN ONE

Can you identify which two items belong to each victim, and which victim may have been the target?

Solution on page 211

# GOLDEN YEARS

**On checking with a** connection at Interpol, you find that Marcellino Gutierrez is a Nicaraguan drug lord, wanted internationally for murder, extortion, smuggling... pretty much everything. And yet here he was, lying underneath a balcony in London Bridge.

Once you bring Derek Rankin in, he folds like a deck of cards, insisting he didn't realize anyone other than the target would die.

He denies having any contact with Unibrow beyond meeting him once in a roadside café to receive the syringe. He went ahead with it because of his debts to organized-crime gangs.

Kempster thinks that's everything, but you don't think he's telling the whole truth and suggest letting him sweat. After half an hour, he admits an extra detail: Unibrow said if Derek could get hold of a key that Gutierrez was holding, he would give him twice the amount. But Derek didn't succeed.

Since you have the key, you get Derek to text Unibrow saying he has it in his possession. It's possible that Unibrow knows Derek has been questioned but, if he really wants the key, he might take the risk anyway. Anyone who would hire Derek is probably not too careful.

Unibrow agrees to meet at the same roadside café in Southwark. You put a monitoring device and a hidden microphone on Derek and escort him there discreetly. You sit in a car opposite the café and watch Derek go in.

Kempster is visibly agitated. "Our boy's not going to be actor of the year, is he? We should abort."

You suggest that Derek's visible anxiety will just seem like he's worried about being caught. Inside the café, Derek greets Unibrow and sits opposite him.

"Let's see it," he says without any greeting.

"OK, here you go. Just give me the money, all right?"

Unibrow sighs. "I need one more favour from you,

Derek. We're going to go together to the locker and you're going to open it."

"What, in case it's booby-trapped?"

"No, of course not! No, listen, it's full of gold sovereigns from... foreign business deals. But I don't like touching gold. I'm allergic or something. I'll pay you directly from what's in there."

Derek clearly distrusts Unibrow but, knowing that we hold the cards, agrees to travel to the storage lockers, which are conveniently nearby. Each locker requires not only the key but for the user to enter an eight-digit code.

"What's the code then?" Derek asks.

"That's the other thing. He never told me. All he ever said was he was a music lover across the centuries, and that he'd had an overture from Tchaikovsky and was going to party like prince. Baffling."

"Who's Tchaikovsky?"

"I dunno. Some rival dealer, I suppose."

You've heard enough and signal the officers nearby to move in. While Derek and Unibrow are bundled into a car, you approach the locker and punch in the code, disgusted that innocent people died because of someone's greed.

## What is the locker code?

Solution on page 211

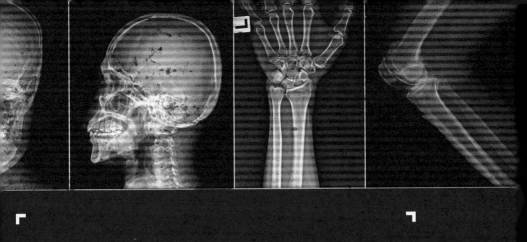

# CSI CHAPTER 7:
# GREAT SNAKES

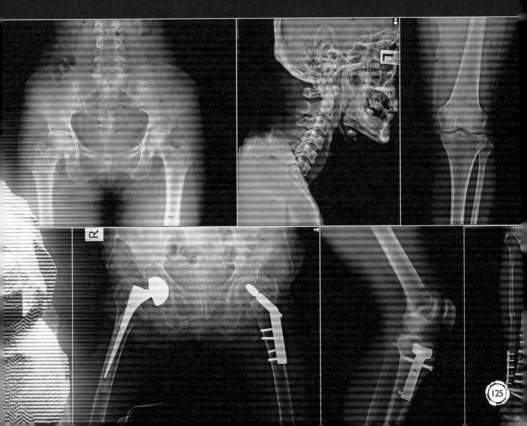

# SITE FOR SORE EYES

**You arrive at the** headquarters in the morning to see Kempster packing up.

"I've been seconded by a crime team in Epsom, Surrey. They need my expertise. There's been an earthquake! And it revealed a body; that's why they need me. You can handle things until I get back."

You point out you have studied seismology, and Kempster eventually agrees you should go with him.

You arrive at the crime scene, which is the site of an archaeological dig, divided up into a grid.

Column clues (top):

```
                                                    2
          3         3  1  1  2            1  1  1
     1       1  2      2  3  3  3  5 11 12    2    4  2  2
     2  1    2  1  2   1  1  2  1  2  2  2 11  7  6  6  3  2  2  2  1
```

Row clues (left):

| Row | Clue |
|-----|------|
| 1 | 1 |
| 2 | 1 |
| 3 | 4,2 |
| 4 | 1,2 |
| 5 | 3,2 |
| 6 | 2,2,1 |
| 7 | 2,2,1 |
| 8 | 3,2,1 |
| 9 | 3,4,1 |
| 10 | 1,7 |
| 11 | 1,6 |
| 12 | 6,1 |
| 13 | 2,6,4 |
| 14 | 7,1 |
| 15 | 1,6,1 |
| 16 | 2,6,1 |
| 17 | 1,3,4,1 |
| 18 | 1,8 |
| 19 | 3,4 |
| 20 | 3 |

## Can you find where the body is?

DC Kempster on his way to Epsom.

Solution on page 211

# TIME JUMP

**The site manager is** an archaeological professor named Simon Klopek, a horrified-looking grey-haired man.

"We thought this might be the site of an Anglo-Saxon burial mound. Then the earthquake happened. We were terrified... and then we found an actual body!"

You decide to save questioning Dr Klopek until he's calmer, and look at the CCTV footage. Around the time of the earthquake, there is a jump cut, as if footage has been removed.

Can you spot the 5 differences between the CCTV image before and after the jump cut?

Solution on page 212

# SIGHT FOR EYESORES

"**It's possible the video** skipped because of the earthquake," Kempster points out.

Now that Klopek is calmer, you get the details. "There were four or five people who were working on site when the earthquake happened; they all moved to protect their work areas and what finds they had."

However, they were all shocked when the body was found.

"It's Solomon Matheson. A local 'eccentric', claimed direct descent from King Frithuwald. He hung around saying his ancestors were unhappy. I think he just wanted attention. He stopped turning up about three months ago."

You speak to the only person who claims to have seen the body being dumped… during the earthquake. She's a tall, thin, elderly lady with a supercilious manner, who peers at you through distinctive blue half-moon glasses.

"Oh yes, I was walking my dog past the dig site. He stopped by number forty-two to do a wee wee, and they had a new sign up, so I took off my distance glasses – they're this lovely pink pair – and put on my reading glasses – they're these semi-circular ones with periwinkle rims – to read it. But then I saw someone peeking out of the front door so I put on my bifocals – they're lovely green horn-rimmed ones I got last Friday. Anyway, then the earth shook and Arnold jumped into my arms and I switched back to my distance glasses – those are the green… sorry, I mean the pink glasses! – and I saw someone throw something big from a passing car. The body."

## Why is she not a reliable witness?

Solution on page 212

# ANCIENT RUINS

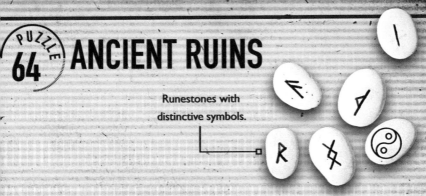

Runestones with
distinctive symbols.

**While the witness's statement** is unreliable, there has definitely been some interference at the site, which all of the archaeologists deny causing. You take them at their word (for now), and check the site for any evidence that seems out of place. The archaeologists beg you to be careful: in part, so you don't disturb their work, and probably also because they don't want you to find anything interesting before they do.

As it happens, you do find something interesting. Floating in a small pool of water in one of the trenches is a series of six perfectly and uniformly round stones, each with distinctive symbols on them.

"Runestones," Kempster says. "I recognize them from my college days. Don't worry, I wasn't a wizard or anything; just used to do role-playing games. You can throw them and use them to predict the future."

You lack knowledge in this area but you're fairly certain the Saxons didn't just scatter runes around their burial mounds. You question the archaeologists to find out if any of them had dug these up already but they all deny it.

"Oh, if I'd found those, I'm sure it'd be the archaeological find of the century," says one generously bearded man in a sarcastic voice, rolling his eyes.

You understand his sarcasm. You're also quite certain that these aren't actual historical artefacts and, in fact, were probably made quite recently.

## What three things make you think these runestones are not historical artifacts?

Solution on page 212

# PRINTING ERROR

Kempster gets out his small portable laboratory and sets it up in one of the site's huts. At first glance, the runes have no trace evidence but, by application of a special mix of chemicals and computer scanning, he manages to pull a partial fingerprint from one of them. It's not one of the archaeologists, so he pulls up a local database.

**Match the partial fingerprint to one of those on the database.**

MATCH

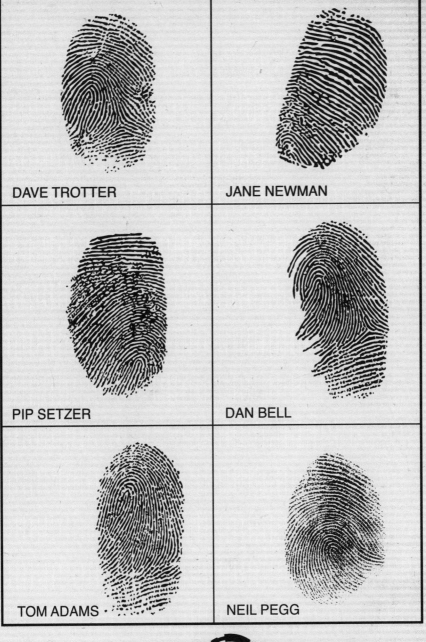

DAVE TROTTER

JANE NEWMAN

PIP SETZER

DAN BELL

TOM ADAMS

NEIL PEGG

Solution on page 212

# PAINT JOB

**Dan Bell lives nearby** in what appears to be a squat. When you arrive, he's headed toward his car, dressed like a cross between a druid and a club DJ, and views you with contempt.

"I don't know anything about a dig," he says. "Now if you'll excuse me…"

"You may not have been there but your car certainly was," says Kempster.

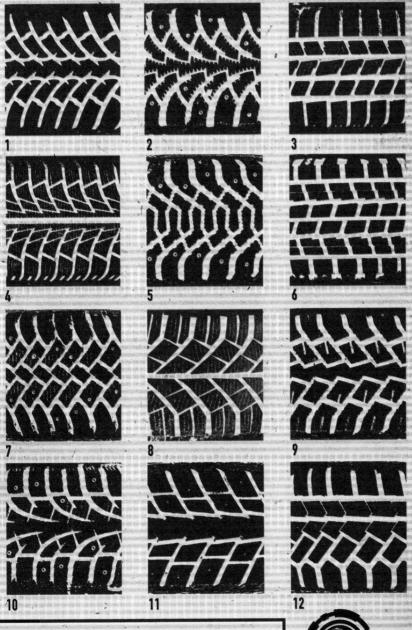

1    2    3

4    5    6

7    8    9

10    11    12

**Which of the twelve tyre treadmarks matches Dan Bell's tyre?**

Solution on page 213

# FRACK STORY

**Dan Bell comes in** for questioning. "I did go to the site. They demeaned Mother Earth with their actions, so I left the stones there!"

You ask him if he knew Solomon Matheson, the man whose body was revealed at the site by the earthquake, and he denies ever meeting him.

Kempster shows you what was in Bell's car. It was full of specialized digging equipment, spades and bags of earth, metal pipes and special probes used to scan for underground metal.

"Who do you work for?" Kempster asks.

Bell swallows. "Middlearth, Inc. They're a local company. They do digging work."

You leave Kempster in the interview and do some research on Middlearth. They're involved in fracking, the process of drilling into the earth then directing a high-pressure water mixture at the rock to release any gas that's inside. A strange job for an "urban druid".

News stories indicate that Middlearth had only begun to explore the possibilities of fracking in Surrey when a court injunction forced them to stop two months ago.

You return to the interview room with this information and Dan Bell reacts with indifference. "Yeah, I just do it for the bread, man, and they've stopped the fracking anyway."

Kempster takes you aside. "So, what do you think? Matheson catches Bell stealing, they fight, Bell hides Matheson's body then tries to come back and get it when the earthquake happened?"

You disagree. You don't think the earthquake was a coincidence.

FRACKING WILL POISON OUR LAND, AIR & WATER

## Why wasn't the earthquake a coincidence?

Solution on page 213

# SOMETHING FISHY

**You take Bell into** custody but don't think he killed Matheson. You don't have enough data yet; there's a big hole at the centre of the case.

Kempster returns from the autopsy on Matheson and says that all evidence suggests he was actually killed off-site and then moved there. He suggests you both check out Matheson's residence.

Matheson lived in a surprisingly large flat in the area. However, head archaeologist Simon Klopek painted an image of Matheson that made him sound like a lunatic who thought Saxon ghosts were unhappy, and his flat seems to bear that out: a dark, cramped labyrinth of old books and strange personal items. The most incongruous element is a huge fish tank in the living room, full of goldfish happily swimming around.

"Did the other archaeologists talk about Matheson?" asks Kempster, taking a sample of the thick layer of dust that has settled on the books.

You tell him that they all agreed that Matheson had been hanging around but that they'd never heard him talk about any Saxon ancestors the way Klopek had claimed.

On searching his kitchen, you find very mouldy bread in the bread bin, and a fridge full of expired food, but no evidence of any murder. It's the same for the bedroom and the bathroom; no signs of any unusual activity.

"This is a bust, I think. No-one's been here for three months," Kempster says.

## You disagree. What indicates someone has visited the flat?

Solution on page 213

# BLURRED TRACES

**There's one door that** you assumed led to a cupboard, but Kempster opens it to find a small photographic dark room, with multiple photos pinned up on a line. Examining the floor, you find a dark patch on the carpet, which luminol reveals to be blood.

"There are five partially developed photos here but only four negatives. One's been… stolen?" Kempster queried.

A

B

C

D

**1**

**4**

**2**

**5**

**3**

Match the negatives to the blurred photos to find which one is missing.

Solution on page 213

# I KNOW THIS FACE

**You find the picture** with no matching negative, but it's too blurry to be any help. However, Kempster fetches his laptop and scans the photo. "I've got pretty good enhancement software," he says. "It's not perfect but it's more discernible. I think these are two of our archaeologists... kissing."

## Which of the archaeologists are kissing in the photo?

MICHELLE ZUNIGER

DOMINIC DA'COSTA

LINUS KNOWLES-SELMAN

KIT MCCANE

SIMON KLOPEK

VLADIMIR ORSON

Solution on page 213

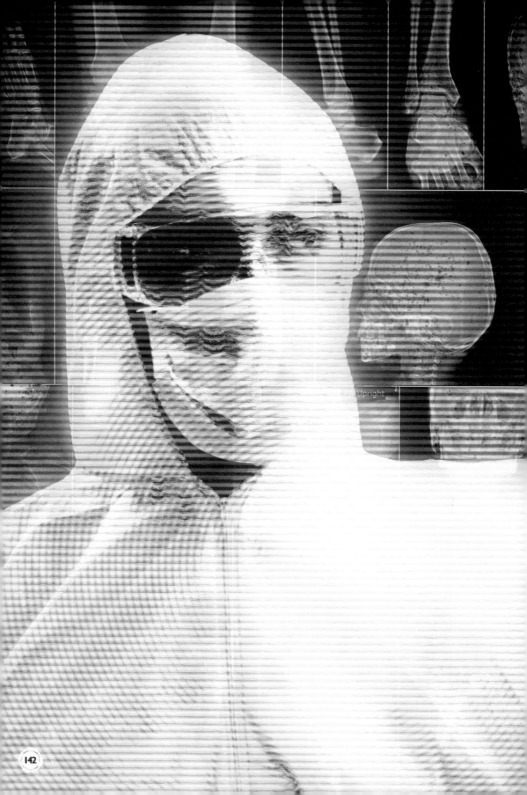

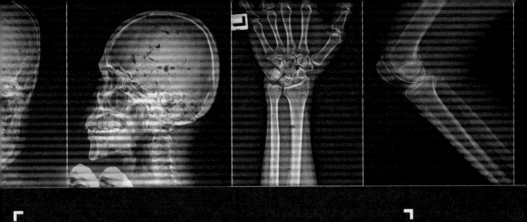

# CSI CHAPTER 8:
## ONLY **GOD**

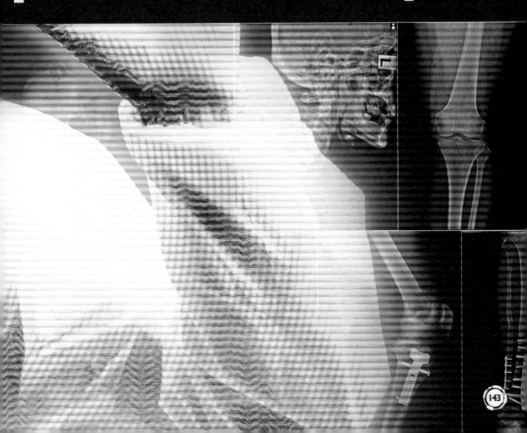

# TRUNK CALL

**You decide to leave** Kempster to his own work and team up with your final suspect, DI Amy Beckhoff. She's no nonsense, very dedicated and appreciates your help.

Your first case is an intriguing one. A pair of woodland hikers cutting through the ancient Gorsebrook Park in Dagenham found a very old, decomposed body with a waterproof backpack in an old bog that was drying out for the first time in decades thanks to the recent hot summers. Even before carbon dating it, you can see a clear way to tell how long the body has been inside hidden.

Based on the objects, how long has the body been hidden?

Solution on page 213

# CLOTHES MAKE THE MAN

**Beckhoff begins filing** relevant paperwork, sends requests for missing-persons details to the central archive, and completes several other administrative tasks that the rest of the detectives tend to leave until later in the case.

"Most people think cold cases mean they can take their time," she says with passion. "But as far as I'm concerned, we should be going twice the speed. The victim's been waiting long enough for justice."

With an eye to speeding the identification process up, she suggests bringing in a particular expert whom she says will be able to pinpoint the victim's death to the year, maybe even the month, without any scientific testing. It sounds dubious to you but you keep your own counsel.

Half an hour later, a glamorous-looking older woman clad in swathes of diaphanous purple fabric arrives at the lab. She introduces herself as Felicity Jude and asks to be shown to the body. For a long, horrifying moment, you think Beckhoff has called in a self-proclaimed psychic or astrologer..

Jude peers at the body and then, with Beckhoff's permission, feels the fabric of its suit, coat and trousers, and even gets Beckhoff to turn the body over so she can examine the collars and cuffs.

She sits and thinks for ten minutes and then stands and says, "I would suggest 1969, probably February based on the cut of the lapels, the thickness of the coat and trousers, the back-stitching… Stripe width is bit variable at this time, wear and tear suggests a work suit, so a front-facing public-service job."

You're relieved. Felicity Jude isn't a psychic at all.

## What is Felicity Jude's profession?

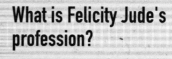

Solution on page 214

# PRET A PUZZLER

**Ms Jude** now produces a set of old catalogues with similar clothing to that of the victim, in the hope that, by pinpointing the manufacturer, they can find the area he's from. There are 15 fashion designers, models, clothes and trends related to the 1960s hidden below.

DEPARTMENT NAME _____    00510450

RECEIPT NO. _____  RECEIVED BY _____  DATE _____
(SIGNATURE)

00510450

```
P A Z M V P N Y L D B F H S D W T B C S
G A T A K U T F L O T J K B C S S O E Y
S Q C N E I Z B M F O H D J L H H T O B
G H E O E R C X E S O E K Y F Y T R P K
I U O D R R S C X C B M U C B O J S K I
Y M Y N S A A N O E O I L R L I S F X S
M E N P C D B L I V G L S U L Y K T Y B
O T J Q N B G A E B O I C O L X U I M M
P R E R M U O F N D G O W V E S U G N M
Q G Q I Q V K W B N V P R K K X J X A I
K Z L D U S T W R Y E U P Z T Q Z R X B
T R I K S I N I M U N C J T Z O Y L G H
P A I S L E Y P P I H C V U Z Q C Y S A
U E C S O W Q O P C Y I T B U T W I F I
H N N C N S W N T M D D E A V W N W N K
D Y Y H D D Y W D J W M N H E I W I H O
S A I N T L A U R E N T D W F G H D R G
Y Y E J Y A X P N S S U O L W G X O B J
N P U D R Y Q C L W G M M Z R Y X K N A
A W E I Q P M L O L N Q E C F V D U S Z
```

## Can you identify them all?

Solution on page 214

# LOGICAL ASSUMPTIONS

**Beckhoff receives the missing-persons** files from the time and finds a few possible candidates. However, the filing system wasn't what it is today and the records have been jumbled. You know the victim was in their twenties.

Mr Palmer was the oldest of the lot and was not down the pub when he was last seen.

The milkman was last seen out on a first date.

The policeman was neither the oldest nor the youngest.

Tom had an interest in flora of all sort from a very young age.

Jack Ryan was last seen on a train to Scotland. It was believed he had crossed the wrong person.

The youngest missing person had been celebrating his 18th birthday at the pub before he went missing.

The 39-year-old was a policeman.

Mr Spurdon neither had an interest in meat, nor was his first name Charlie.

The man last seen at the shop was a 62-year-old banker who had recently had some rather unfortunate marital problems.

Bill's last name was neither Palmer nor Perrier and he was older than Jack Ryan.

Mr Perrier was not 29 when he went missing.

## Can you work out who the missing person was, their job, and where they were last seen?

| | Palmer | Perrir | Ryan | Spurdon | Thompson | Last seen on date | Last seen meeting supplier | Last seen at pub | Last seen at shop | Last seen on train | Banker | Butcher | Gardener | Milkman | Policeman | 18 | 29 | 39 | 43 | 62 |
|---|---|---|---|---|---|---|---|---|---|---|---|---|---|---|---|---|---|---|---|---|
| Bill | | | | | | | | | | | | | | | | | | | | |
| Charlie | | | | | | | | | | | | | | | | | | | | |
| Jack | | | | | | | | | | | | | | | | | | | | |
| Ted | | | | | | | | | | | | | | | | | | | | |
| Tom | | | | | | | | | | | | | | | | | | | | |
| 18 | | | | | | | | | | | | | | | | | | | | |
| 29 | | | | | | | | | | | | | | | | | | | | |
| 39 | | | | | | | | | | | | | | | | | | | | |
| 43 | | | | | | | | | | | | | | | | | | | | |
| 62 | | | | | | | | | | | | | | | | | | | | |
| Banker | | | | | | | | | | | | | | | | | | | | |
| Butcher | | | | | | | | | | | | | | | | | | | | |
| Gardener | | | | | | | | | | | | | | | | | | | | |
| Milkman | | | | | | | | | | | | | | | | | | | | |
| Policeman | | | | | | | | | | | | | | | | | | | | |
| Last seen on date | | | | | | | | | | | | | | | | | | | | |
| Last seen meeting supplier | | | | | | | | | | | | | | | | | | | | |
| Last seen at pub | | | | | | | | | | | | | | | | | | | | |
| Last seen at shop | | | | | | | | | | | | | | | | | | | | |
| Last seen on train | | | | | | | | | | | | | | | | | | | | |

Solution on page 214

# YOU BET

**Found near the body** was a betting slip from the famous Dagenham Dog Track – now closed but, in the sixties, a popular venue.

"Do you think his bet won? If so, that's money worth killing for," says Beckhoff, sending a request for records of the races.

| RACE 1 | RACE 2 | RACE 3 | RACE 4 |
|---|---|---|---|
| Stinky Jim | Disparate Dan | Frank the Yank | Pulsator |
| Bright Lightning | Vorpal Sword | Middle Road | Box Smart |
| W: Grey Magic 5-1 | Not A Wolf | Hit the Heights | W: Spider Girl 4-1 |
| Born Slippy | Dingo Starr | Natterjack Smith | Pince Nez |
| 2: Spotty Rick 3-1 | W: Glengarry 2-5 on | 2: Doris Daze 2-1 | Flower Child |
| Destiny's Child | 2: Tripod 4-1 | Red Smudge | Fox Chaser |
| Smithereens | Todhunter's Folly | W: Phil the Flyer 20-1 | Champagne Carly |
| Colonel Goodlegs | Secretariat The Dog | Pen Name | 2: Finky 30-1 |

| RACE 5 | RACE 6 |
|---|---|
| Mint Cake | White Caviar |
| Duck Livers | Steve |
| W: Miranda Panda 16-3 | Brigadoon |
| Fill the Greek | Novelty Bobble |
| Tanker Top | Churchill's Pride |
| Blue Bayou | W: Immaculate Pasta 3-1 |
| 2: Assassin 1-2 on | Mr The Price |
| Pointless Pup | 2: Gusto 7-2 |

Billy Brooks Betting Shop
SJ £1 to win. Dingo Starr £2 each way. P the F £10 to win. FC £1 each way. PP £1 to win. IP £2 to win.

Solution on page 214

**Looking at the records, can you discover how much money the betting slip was worth?**

# PUZZLE 76 DNA DILEMMA

"**The victim's** name is Ted Spurdon. He was reported missing on 17 February 1969 by his mother, Doris. He was 29, worked as a milkman, went on a date and never came home. His date claimed he'd ditched her after half an hour. Both the mum and the date are now dead – I checked. Natural causes."

Beckhoff paces the room, writing a few task lists as she does so.

"We need to quickly find out if he has any living relatives. But it's been so long since that time and we need to move quickly. We could use social media, genealogy databases that people upload their DNA to, maybe put out a press release or some kind of appeal, get other areas of the department on it…"

As she paces, you notice a door in her laboratory that you've never been through. In fact, large parts of the building haven't been in use for a while, probably either due to renovation or budget cuts. But, out of curiosity, you go to open the door. Beckhoff darts forward and stops you, with a look of slight panic in her eyes.

"STOP!"

She suddenly looks self-conscious and withdraws her hand. "That area, uh, it's full of asbestos. They keep promising to clear it out but it's a bureaucratic nightmare. Best not go in there."

She steeples her fingers. "What's the best way to do track down his family now?"

## Which of the options Beckhoff has listed would be the fastest place to start?

Solution on page 215

# SHORTCUTS

**You find he has a** sister, Emily, now 72 and living in sheltered accomodation in Brighton. She's a sprightly little lady with a distinctive beehive hairdo, and very happy to help.

"Ooh, Ted? Well, I remember me Mum being well upset when he went missing. But I never actually met him. You see, he was me half-brother, and there was bad blood. I would've loved to have known him. I didn't even live in that area, love."

Beckhoff shakes her head. "Stop lying."

## How did Beckhoff know Emily was lying?

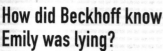

Solution on page 215

# MEMORY LANE

**Emily is surprised.** "Ooh, my word. I'd forgotten that. 1969, was it? Oh yes. Sorry, me old memory's not what it was. Half of the time, I don't know what day it is, let alone remember things fifty years ago! Sorry, dearies."

You notice a book of cryptic crosswords in the corner of the room, and pick it up.

"Oh those?" says Emily. "Left over from the previous resident, I think. Don't have the heart to chuck 'em out."

Further inquiries get a similar response, before you notice one of the care workers hovering nearby. He motions you over; Beckhoff stays with Emily.

"I heard what she said. Don't believe a word of it from that one," he says. "She's got a memory like a steel trap – every single tiny mistake any care worker has made, she keeps in a list in her head!"

Hastily, he adds, "Except me. I don't make mistakes."

You return to Beckhoff and Emily, and decide to see who's being truthful.

"Emily, can I ask you a question?"

"Sure, love."

"Listen carefully. A man named Cosmo went shopping. At the greengrocer, he bought lettuce; at the butcher, he bought trout; at the newsagent, he bought *The Times*; at the florist, he bought some petunias; and at the dressmaker's, he bought a thimble. Can you tell me what his shopping list was?"

Emily smiles. "Oh, I'm sorry, dear, I told you about me memory; I don't remember anything of what Cosmo bought."

You have your answer.

Petunias

*Times* newspaper

Lettuce

Trout

Thimble

## Have you proved she has a good memory?

# ONCE BITTEN

**Beckhoff gets a message** on her phone. Kempster has completed the autopsy. He says Ted Spurdon died from a blow to the head with a heavy object, causing a brain haemorrhage, but that there is also evidence of human bite marks on his forearm.

You get Kempster to send you the pictures, and you go to see the care worker. "You don't have any dental records for Emily, do you?"

"As it happens…"

He leads you to the administrative office and pulls a series of x-rays. To your dismay, they don't match the bite marks, but then you are struck by a thought. These x-rays are only from the past couple of years, while Emily has been in care. Perhaps her older records will tell a different tale.

What's more, the care worker's grudge runs deep, and he is willing to track down her original entry files, which lists her old dentist. You hurry over and gain access to Emily's x-rays from decades ago.

## Can you spot the eight differences between her oldest x-ray and her most recent one?

The care worker, fortuitously helpful.

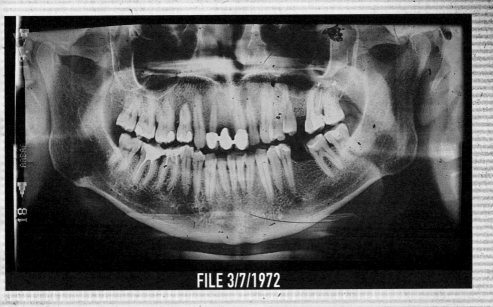

FILE 3/7/1972

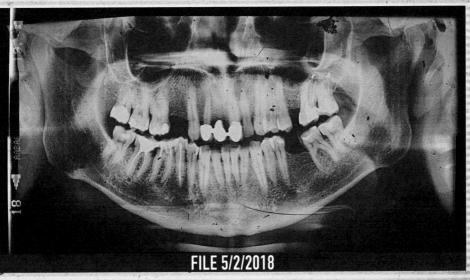

FILE 5/2/2018

Solution on page 215

155

# ANOTHER FAMILY TREE

**You talk to Emily** about the bite marks and she bursts into tears, confessing everything. Ted had arranged to meet her in Gorsebrook Park, just to talk, she thought, but he tried to assault her. She fought back, biting him and he fell smashed his head against a rock on the ground. Panicking, she pushed his body into the bog and ran home, assuming he would be found, but he never was and, as the years rolled by, she went into denial about the whole thing.

You consult with Beckhoff.

"The bite-marks are definitely consistent with self-defence," she says. "And his mother's missing-persons report did imply he was a bit of a nasty piece of work, as did his date's statement."

However, you say, "Yes, but the missing £200. And is it likely that a person of Emily's stature could push a body deep enough into a bog to hide it like that on her own? If you won £200 at the dogs, would your first act be to meet your half-sister in a park, or would it be to go and get rat... get drunk?"

You decide to interview Emily back at headquarters in a more formal setting. She's still tearful but a lot more guarded. You ask her about the missing money.

"Oh, I didn't know anything about that."

"You're sure you didn't take it? Spend it? No one would blame you," says Beckhoff, trying to appear to be on her side.

"If I'd had £100, it would have changed me life. But I had no idea about it."

You look over at Beckhoff. You hadn't mentioned any amount of money.

## Why would she say £100 when £200 was stolen?

DI Beckhoff,
unconvinced.

Solution on page 215

PA Upright

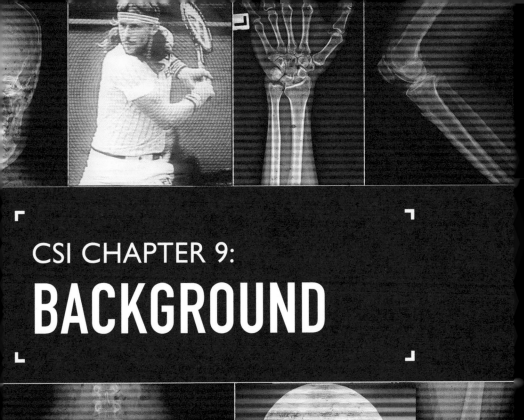

# CSI CHAPTER 9:
# BACKGROUND

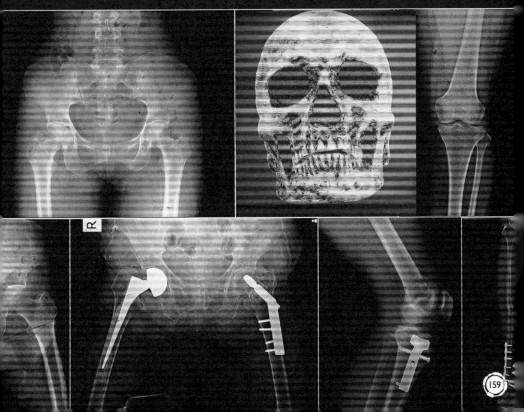

# PANAMA GUZZLER

Online celebrity:
Zinc Tooth AKA
Rebecca Terbot.

**Beckhoff barely has** time to take a breath before she's assigned her next case. After solving a mystery over 50 years old, you're now thrown into a crime that's still happening: a young online celebrity known as Zinc Tooth (real name Rebecca Terbot) has been kidnapped! After she disappeared, her parents received a distorted ransom call in the form of an audio file anonymously sent to their email, demanding one million pounds. The Met's Kidnap Unit wants your help to uncover anything that could possibly help them find her. You travel to the parents' house, which has been set up as a hub for the rescue operation.

Before you listen to the recording, you talk to her parents. Jane and Noel Terbot are unassuming middle-class people, the only unusual thing about them being their matching blonde hair and striking blue eyes. They are both mid-level office workers and seem equally as baffled by their daughter's online fame as her being kidnapped. They're rattled but coping.

"She said she was going to film a video over at a friend's house. We didn't question it – she's so independent," said Jane. "But then we didn't hear from her and nobody had seen her… And then we got that message…"

Sobbing, she hugs her husband, who seems on the brink of tears himself.

"We don't have a million pounds, Miss Beckhoff," says Noel. "We don't even own this house. What are we going to do?"

As Beckhoff extracts what little information Jane and Noel Terbot have, you look around their place in the hope that it may hold some clues or evidence of her disappearance. The Terbots are not suspects as such but, in these situations, you have to entertain all possibilities.

Their house is clean and could have come out of a catalogue for people who like Swedish furniture and have little imagination. The only touches of real individuality come from what you assume are their daughter's flourishes, from a wall covered in plastic doughnuts to a "selfie tent" in the corridor. There's also

a large framed print of a newspaper article about anarchists bombing an unoccupied post office in Sweden in 1987. No one was harmed but the suspects, Markus and Alice Borett, were still at-large. A strange thing for a teenager to like but you can't account for taste.

You return to the couple. Beckhoff is working out the timeline of the kidnap. "When you received the audio file, you waited for about a day before you contacted us. Why is that?"

"Well… it told us not to contact the police," explains Noel, "and I mean, you know, we were worried about her getting hurt."

Beckhoff shoots you a look. The audio never mentioned not contacting the police. It's implied, certainly. But you think there might be another reason why they would be reluctant to involve the police.

# Why would the girl's parents be reluctant to involve police in their life?

Solution on page 216

# WAVE OF THE FUTURE

**Your realisation about** the parents might be relevant to the case but you decide not to question them about it yet. Instead, you and Beckhoff start analyzing the sound file. There's an indistinct sound in the background of the recording…Beckhoff has isolated the moment it occurs.

CAR HORN

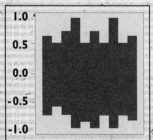

ELEPHANT

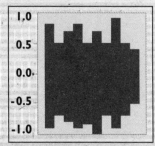

GUNSHOT

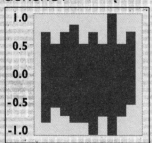

SNEEZE

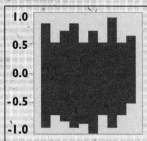

TAPE

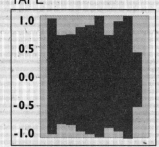

Can you determine which sound is in the background of the tape from these four stock recordings you have on file?

Solution on page 216

# CAR NOISES

**Beckhoff highlights another background** sound on the recording. It's faint but more easily discernible – a level and muted steady vibration. It's a car engine, idling somewhere and being repeatedly revved, as if someone is testing it.

Cars are obviously everywhere but, at this point, anything's a potential clue. You turn to Beckhoff. "I think we should—"

"Contact a car expert and get them to assess the sound to see if they can identify what type of engine it is? I'm in touch with one right now."

Minutes later, you are on a video call with the Met's resident car expert, Valentino "Ears" Earhart. You play it to him over the microphone but it's a little too faint.

"I can't hear anything. And for me, that's tough. Can you send me the clip?"

"We'll try but time's a real factor here, Ears. Can you give us an idea of what to listen for?"

"I reckon it could be any one of a V8, straight-six or a diesel. A V8 is a loud rumbling, like someone gargling with marbles. A straight-six is softer and smoother, like a cat purring in a cardboard box. And a diesel is clunkier, like a spinning top in a plastic bucket."

With this in mind, you play the clip again. After listening closely, you think you know what type of engine it is.

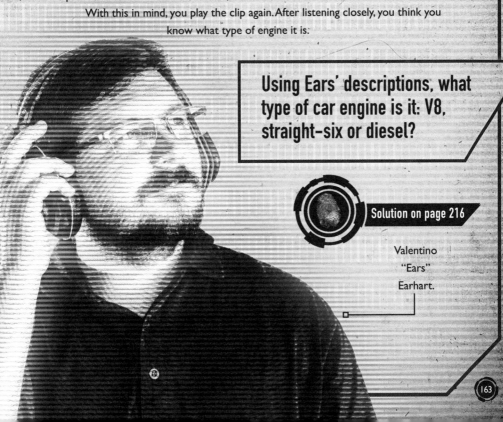

**Using Ears' descriptions, what type of car engine is it: V8, straight-six or diesel?**

Solution on page 216

Valentino
"Ears"
Earhart.

# DING DONG

**You identify a third background** sound, which is a church bell. Then you get notification from Aksoy that the anonymous email's IP number tracks it to the Tower Hamlets area, which is notorious for its abundance of churches, auto repair shops and large animal centres like urban farms and zoos. There is only one street within easy hearing of each, though – Meteor Street. Your audio technicians begin to work on evaluating the strengths of each sound.

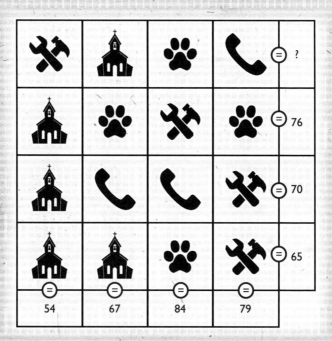

Can you find each sound's value, and add them together to find the correct street number?

**Solution on page 216**

# LABYRINTH

**You, Beckhoff and the** Kidnap Unit rush to the location, sirens blazing.

When you arrive, you find the front door of the house open. The place is in a state of disarray, the building a network of rat-like tunnels made by huge stacks of newspapers all along the walls. You see a trail of blood at the doorstep and begin following it to its source.

START

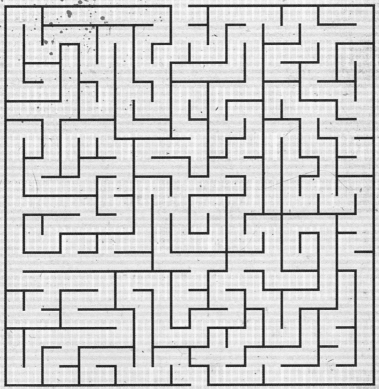

FINISH

## Find your way through the maze.

Solution on page 217

# HOUSE OF LOVE

**You find Rebecca Terbot** shivering in the cupboard, with haunted eyes and a big cut on her arm but otherwise unharmed.

Once you've extracted her from the house and given her a blanket and a cup of tea, she's able to tell her story. She was on her way to a friend's house when a van screeched to a halt next to her and unseen hands grabbed her and threw her in the back. She was driven to an unknown location, where she was kept tied up somewhere, then thrown into a car boot and driven here. During the second trip, her blindfold ripped so she could see, but her captor wore a facemask, so she never saw his real face. (One of the SOCOs finds it inside: it's a rubber mask of Bjorn Borg.)

"'This place is weird,' I thought. 'It's completely full of old magazines called things like *Deuce* and *Volley Times*,'" Rebecca explains. "Anyway, I managed to move the chair over to the window and broke off a bit of wood, and used it to cut the ropes. Then, the next time he came, I made a run for it, but he grabbed me. He was very strong; his right arm was really muscular, though his left was a lot weaker. Anyway, we struggled and he stabbed me with the wood, but I managed to break away and hide. He never came after me though. I heard him running off and calling someone, saying, 'She slipped the net!'"

You ask if she has any idea who he is.

"Nope. But he was pretty fit, and I've been doing a series of comedy videos with sports people, I did one with a footballer, a tennis player, a golfer and a swimmer."

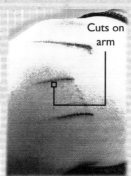

Cuts on arm

## Which sportsperson do you think kidnapped Rebecca?

Solution on page 217

# IF THE SHOE FITS

**While the Kidnap Unit** takes Rebecca back home, you find shoe prints on the floor of the house. You take a scan of them and compare them to common brands of sports shoes to find a match.

## Which print is the odd one out?

Solution on page 217

# ELEMENTARY

**Back at the lab,** you're given the shirt Rebecca was wearing when she was kidnapped.

EVENTS:

1. Grabbed and thrown into a builder's van.

2. Tied up at first location.

3. Thrown into a car boot.

4. Tied up in the second house.

5. Gets cut and escapes.

Wet paper and ink

Sawdust

Plastic fibres from nylon rope

Grease from tyre jack

Blood stain

## There are five significant stains on Rebecca's shirt. Can you match each one to the event that caused it?

Solution on page 218

# PUZZLE 89 ANYONE FOR TENNIS

**You visit Rebecca back** at her house with her parents. You've decided not to pursue their possible past crimes as you feel it's irrelevant to the case and you have much bigger fish to fry. They all seem very happy and relieved. You decide to question Rebecca further about the tennis comedy video she made.

"Oh yeah, well, it's this whole series about me working with sports people to try to get good at their sport, but really I'm just messing about and being silly and bad at it – people love that stuff. But the tennis guy, John Macsomething, was definitely not into it."

"Did he seem agitated or upset?"

"Yeah. Not at first, but when I was holding the tennis bat the wrong way up, he started getting very annoyed. He kept saying he couldn't believe I made so much money pretending to be stupid, and then, when I tried to score a tennis goal with the stumps instead of the ball, he said I was stupid and asked where I'd got the stumps from."

"But he did do the video?"

"Yeah, he said he had big debts, otherwise there's no way he'd work with someone like me. And when I thought I'd got a strike and ran around the pitch with my shirt over my head I could see him staring evils at me, but in a really calculated way. At the end, when I told him I didn't lose the match because I had an extra life, he threw his tennis bat all the way over a fence and we decided it was time to go."

# What six mistakes has Rebecca made about tennis that infuriated the tennis player?

Solution on page 218

# YOU'RE THE VOICE

**You bring in the suspect,** a formerly famous tennis player who has fallen upon rough times. You suggest taking him to one of the alternative interrogation suites that you know is a little bit shabbier, to try to rattle him, but Beckhoff quickly cuts you off, saying that it's "...unavailable. They had to close it because of the rats."

"Not the asbestos?"

"Well, the rats have been eating the asbestos. It's made them very cranky."

The tennis player has a cheap lawyer with him and declares he knows nothing about any of this.

You play him the audio the parents were sent just after their daughter went missing, with the distorted, disguised voice saying, "Listen. We have your daughter. You will pay us one million of pounds or she will die. In anguish and pain. Do not mess with us. Further details will be forthcoming." He admits to having made the video with her, but says if everyone who's annoyed at a teenager can be accused of kidnapping them, you'd have almost everyone over 25 in jail right now.

"Listen. You cannot be serious about this! Unless you can prove I was anywhere near that weird house, or this van I'm supposed to have, or anything else to do with this case, I'm walking right now and then suing your asses for persecution and wrongful accusation."

While Beckhoff is talking to him, you check his shoes against the prints you found at the site but there's no match, and there's no evidence anywhere of him owning or even ever visiting the magazine-filled house, and no record of him owning a white builder's van.

Back in the interview suite, he's being increasingly belligerent. "I don't need a million of pounds anyway! I've got a forthcoming exhibition match against Pete Sampras that's going to pay a lot of money."

He leans forward and stares at Beckhoff. "Listen. You're causing me and my family a lot of anguish and pain with this. Drop it."

Beckhoff and you let him leave for now, and you go to the lab with the recording of his voice to see if it matches the one on the recording. But the distortional disguise is so effective that, even if it is him, there's no way to match it.

"It's game over for now unless we find some other physical evidence," suggests Beckhoff.

But you don't think so. You think there's a way of proving that it's his voice on the recording without matching the exact wavelength…, because there's another way to show that what he says matches the kidnapper's voice.

**What three things give away that it is his voice on the audio file?**

Mr. Macsomething.
Not playing ball.

Solution on page 218

PA Upright

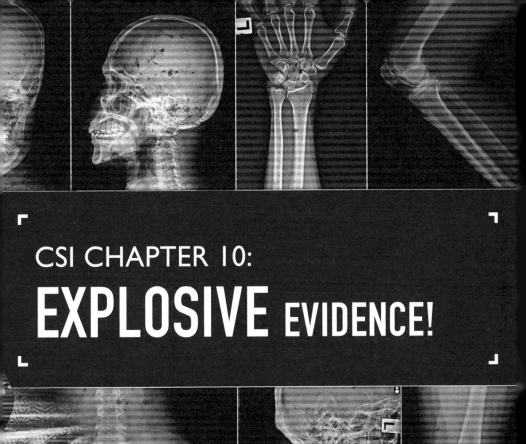

# CSI CHAPTER 10:
# EXPLOSIVE EVIDENCE!

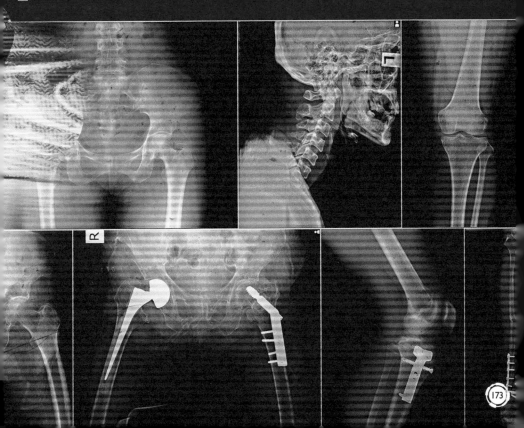

# SAMPLE CASE

**Beckhoff is uncharacteristically** nervous: She's presenting evidence at the Old Bailey for the prosecution case of Michael Bridger, gangland kingpin and possibly a high-ranking member of SW1X. The CPS are hoping he'll flip and name names but, so far, he's not budging. Beckhoff is packing up her samples but needs to ensure that no two similar samples are touching to avoid cross contamination.

## How can you fill the grid so that no two similar samples are in the same row, column or bold 3x3 box?

Solution on page 218

# POP QUIZ

**You arrive at the Old Bailey,** the world-famous courthouse in the City of London, and pass through security before entering the special waiting room where Kempster and Aksoy are already standing with their own evidence.

Kempster seems surprisingly chipper. "Nice day for justice!" he says, and you can't tell if he's being sarcastic or not. Then he excuses himself to go to the toilet.

Aksoy comes over chummily. "The Old Bailey's corridors still have all the classical architecture, but once you get in the courtroom, it's like a little beige box. Not like on TV at all. And I should know!"

He suddenly looks guilty. "Because... I watch a lot of TV."

Beckhoff looks increasingly worried. "This court case steps on the toes of Operation Guineafowl, the smash-and-grab that Vernon was investigating when he was murdered. If I accidentally let slip any details about that during this, it'll compromise the other ongoing investigation and possibly cause a mistrial! Can we run through some of the details?"

**Question 1.** What was the name of the man who owned the warehouse?

**Question 2.** What is the name of the organized crime gang who you think did the robbery and is possibly in control of the infiltrator?

**Question 3.** Are the warehouse workers
A) Vegetarian
B) Pescatarian
C) Vegan?

**Question 4.** What was the name of the café where the robbers ate?

**Question 5.** What was the name of the gang member who was murdered on the roof of a pub?

**Solution on page 219**

# CROSS EXAMINER

**Beckhoff is first** questioned by the prosecution, before she is cross-examined by Bridger's defence lawyer, a menace named Lucian Jones who's demolished witnesses before. She remains stone-faced under his barrage of questions. He implies that his client is innocent and that, somehow, Beckhoff herself was responsible for the crime: an elaborate diamond heist.

"You said to my learned colleague that you analyzed the samples of dirt found at the scene and that they matched samples of dirt found on shoes located at the house of Mr Bridger."

"That is correct."

"And yet you didn't find similar samples on the other shoes in the closet, despite the fact that they would have been in close proximity and had not been stored with care. I find it more likely that the shoes and samples came into contact while in your lab—"

"Objection, My Lady. There's no proof of that being the case," interrupts the prosecution counsel.

The judge leans forward. "Do you have any proof of this, Mr Jones?"

Jones sniffs. "My lady, the police unit that DI Beckhoff works for has caused a previous case to collapse due to shoddy evidence handling. Seeing as my client has been proved to be in Toronto in the US at the time of the crime, and only returned from there two weeks after, it seems unlikely his shoes would have been anywhere near the crime scene."

Unlikely as it seems, Jones just made a big error – although not one that will lose him the case.

## What was Jones's error?

Solution on page 219

# A BRIDGER TOO FAR

**Aksoy enters the court** and whispers something in your ear that you really didn't expect. "We have to evacuate. There's been a bomb threat!"

Making your way out of the court, you notice two security guards are missing.

"They both ran for the loo," says Aksoy. "Very strange. Can you take custody of Bridger? We need to find out what's happening." Aksoy and Beckhoff leave.

You stand with Bridger but suddenly realize you also have to look after a powerful electromagnet that is one of the pieces of evidence, and a laptop Beckhoff was using. You get a call saying you need to transfer all three to the secure zone in the adjacent hallway, but the narrow security door means you can only transfer one thing through at a time. If you leave Bridger with the electromagnet, he might use it to disable the building's security and escape. But if you leave the electromagnet with the laptop, it might activate and wipe the laptop's important contents.

## What series of steps do you need to take to ensure that Bridger and the two pieces of evidence stay intact?

Solution on page 219

# SHORT CIRCUIT COURT

**Now that you are** securely outside the danger zone, Aksoy appears holding, for some reason, a game-console controller. He gestures at it. "This is the controller for Johnny 6 – it's a bomb-disposal robot. Security here have confirmed there's an actual device inside, so we're going to send this guy in to take a look. What we need to do is work out the series of concise movements to get it to the bomb. Any wrong steps and it could get stuck.

START

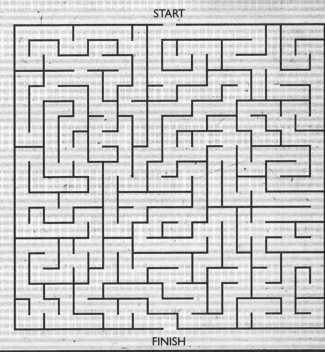

FINISH

## Can you find your way through the maze without taking any wrong turns, doubling back on yourself or taking your pencil off the page?

Solution on page 219

# HAVE A HEART

**The robot makes** it to the device and, using the built-in camera, Aksoy confirms that there's a real IED (improvised explosive device) in the courtroom, nestled among dropped papers and a bunch of angina capsules that a running barrister accidentally spilled.

Beckhoff joins you while Aksoy continues to talk.

"This robot's a little pet project of mine. It was a medical robot, believe it or not, designed to help people with heart conditions! I redesigned it; equipped it with sample-gathering equipment. I can extract air from around the bomb and test it electronically to get an idea of what explosive materials they've used and, therefore, how powerful a blast we're looking at."

He activates the device and Johnny 6 begins hoovering molecules from around the device.

"There are a few options here," continues Aksoy. "Could be PE4 – that's plastic explosive – or TNT – mostly used in mining – or even nitro-glycerine. That's nasty stuff but they give it to people with heart problems. I always think of the chemical structure of nitro-glycerine as being like if Santa Claus was blown up! 'Ho, ho, oh no! BOOM!'"

Beckhoff shoots him a steely look. He continues looking at the screen.

"And here are the results," he says. "Hmm… It's detecting both plastic explosives AND nitro-glycerine. That's weird. How is that possible?"

## Why did the robot detect two explosive chemicals?

Solution on page 220

**Aksoy focuses the camera**

"Believe it or not, we've got to cut the right wire. We need the one that feeds to the triggering device. If we cut the power source or the explosive wire, it might be booby-trapped."

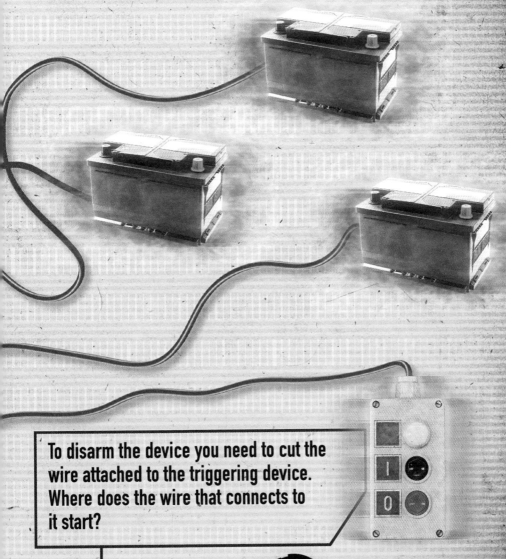

To disarm the device you need to cut the wire attached to the triggering device. Where does the wire that connects to it start?

Solution on page 220

# EXTREMELY MISTRUSTFUL TECHNICIAN

**With the device successfully** disarmed, Aksoy begins the process of carefully dismantling it with the robot. Meanwhile, Beckhoff is handling the evacuation with the building's remaining security.

"They've no idea how the device got into the building. I think we can all assume why. Either to disrupt the court case, or literally to blow up evidence, witnesses, maybe Bridger himself. If his bosses thought he would flip, I wouldn't put it past them to blow him up."

A scattered bunch of lawyers and witnesses from other cases are uncertain what happens next: do they go back into their courts? Beckhoff continues reassuring them and telling them to wait for more information when a man cries out. He'd banged his foot running out of his courtroom and is now experiencing extreme pain.

"Excuse me, does anyone have any medical training here?" asks Beckhoff, as she notices a gentleman sidling away who is wearing the uniform of an EMT. She beckons him over and he carefully inspects the man who is crying out.

"It's just a pulled… ligament," the EMT says haltingly. "If he rests it and puts ice on it, it'll be fine."

"Are you the court's EMT?" Beckhoff asks.

"Er, no, I'm here to be a witness. I'll be evacuated with the others, right?"

"Yes, probably. Is this your first time being involved with a bomb?"

The EMT looks scared, then relaxes. "Oh, oh yes. It was scary. As scary as the time a guy was having a heart attack and I had to use the defibrillators to give him a cardiac arrest."

Beckhoff smiles and nods. As the EMT walks off, she moves carefully to you and says, "Get security to seal the exits. That man's not an EMT. He might be our bomber."

## How does Beckhoff know the man isn't an emergency medical technician?

**Solution on page 220**

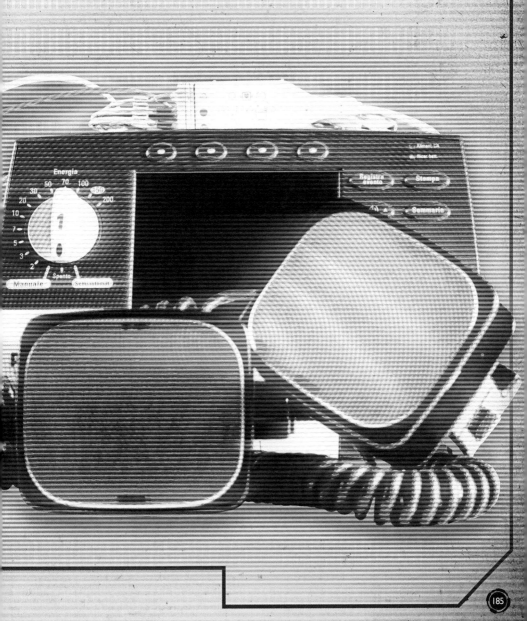

# BOMBER RUN

**As soon as he** realizes he's been detected, the bomber takes off at speed, running through the maze of corridors.

# Can you track him?

Solution on page 220

# SANCTUARY

**You arrive at the basement** to find... nobody. He's disappeared.

"How is that possible?" Beckhoff asks, enraged.

Then you remember something from your old lectures. The Old Bailey has a secret tunnel that connects to...

"St Sepulchre's Church!" you shout, and you both run.

St Sepulchre's is opposite the Old Bailey and is a large Gothic church with an imposing tower. As soon as you get inside, you spot the bomber, sitting in the pews almost casually. As you approach him carefully, he looks up and smiles.

"Tough luck, coppers. You can't arrest me here. I claim the ancient right of sanctuary! That's correct: I can remain here and you can't remove me from the church."

You're about to point out that the right to sanctuary ended in the seventeenth century, but Beckhoff makes a big show of punching the air and saying, "DAMMIT! You're right!" and then looks you in the eye, silently warning you not to say anything.

She sits next to the bomber. "Man, you're clever. I never would have thought of that. We can't touch you now."

The bomber smiles. "Yeah, I remembered it from this TV show I watched. So you might as well go now. I'm not going anywhere."

"Well, seeing as we can't arrest you, can you at least tell us why you planted the bomb?"

The bomber shrugs. "I guess I can. I owed money to this bloke in SWIX. He told me where I needed to plant it, got me the costume, even gave me the bomb! I said, 'How am I going to get it in there?' and he said someone in the building would help me; that I could pass it to him through a window, a blind spot in the security."

Beckhoff nods and smiles. "Can you tell us anything about this person?"

The bomber shakes his head. "Not really. I didn't even see him, and then once I got inside, he'd just left the bomb in the stall. It could have even been a woman! Then I hid it in the courtroom. I had no idea you'd have robots and everything."

"Were you told to detonate the bomb?" she asks, as a couple of police officers entered the church at the other end.

"Yeah, but only once I was sure that Bridger bloke was in the building, and

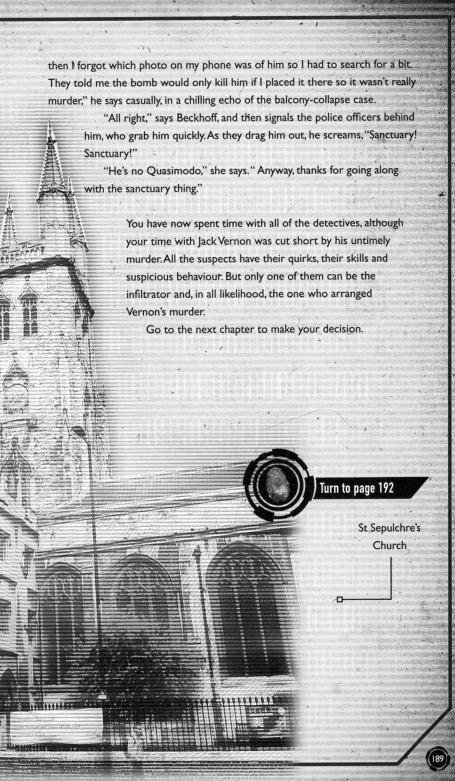

then I forgot which photo on my phone was of him so I had to search for a bit. They told me the bomb would only kill him if I placed it there so it wasn't really murder," he says casually, in a chilling echo of the balcony-collapse case.

"All right," says Beckhoff, and then signals the police officers behind him, who grab him quickly. As they drag him out, he screams, "Sanctuary! Sanctuary!"

"He's no Quasimodo," she says. "Anyway, thanks for going along with the sanctuary thing."

You have now spent time with all of the detectives, although your time with Jack Vernon was cut short by his untimely murder. All the suspects have their quirks, their skills and suspicious behaviour. But only one of them can be the infiltrator and, in all likelihood, the one who arranged Vernon's murder.

Go to the next chapter to make your decision.

**Turn to page 192**

St Sepulchre's
Church

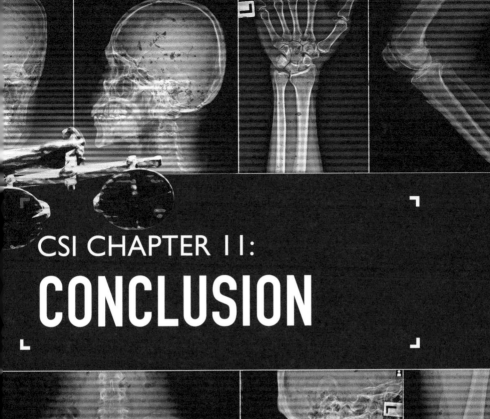

# CSI CHAPTER 11:
# CONCLUSION

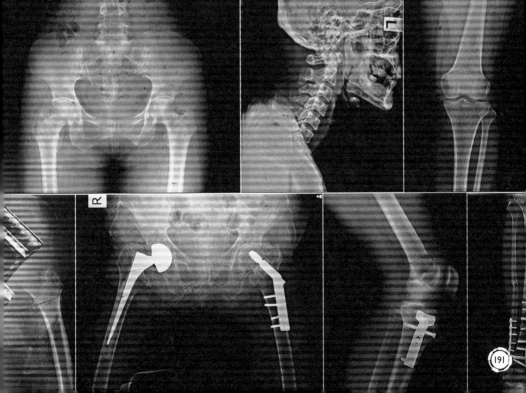

# ? DECISION TIME

**Who do you think is the traitor?**

If you think it is
DI Dustin Aksoy,
turn to page 221

If you think it is
DI Abigail Beckhoff,
turn to page 222

If you think it is
DI Kelvin Kempster,
turn to page 223

If you think it is
DI Jack Vernon
(DECEASED)

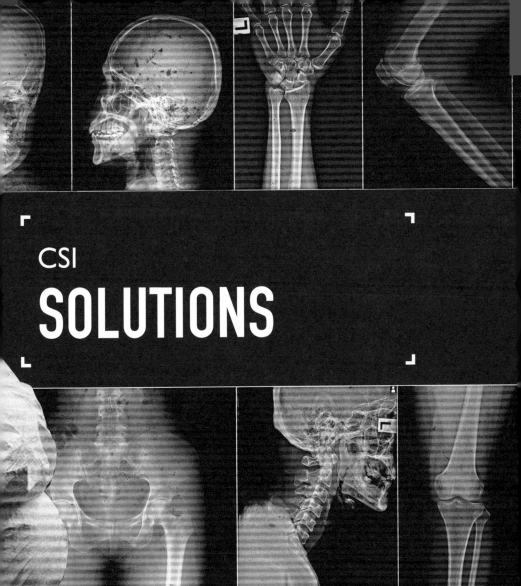

# CSI
# SOLUTIONS

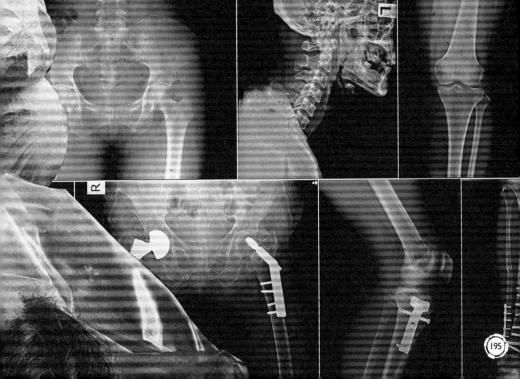

**01**

Aksoy is a player of the popular miniature war-gaming pastime "StarAttack 50,000" and the emails are orders for new figures, plastic weapons, etc., and his latest planned moves in coordination with other players. The money is because this hobby is very expensive. The emails are encrypted because, despite his general informality, even Aksoy realizes he shouldn't be playing games at work.

**02**

The landlady has Obsessive Compulsive Disorder and, after finding the body, was so distressed that she couldn't keep herself from tidying his room. She felt so guilty that she couldn't bring herself to confess. She cleans the corridors compulsively, straightens and smooths her dress and repeatedly flicks the light switch, which are all common signs of OCD.

**03**

A raven. All the others are allusions to chess pieces: a KINGfisher, a Yellow BISHOP, a ROOK, and a (K)NIGHTjar.

**04**

1 – The Super Mario Brothers.   2 – The Everly Brothers.
3 – Big Brother.   4 – *O Brother, Where Art Thou?*.
5 – The Brothers Grimm.   Connection: They're all about brothers.

**05**

She was looking up details about him on the internet, using her phone. That's why she kept looking at it and stopped when her battery ran out.

```
C C T T G A A C T T C T G T A T C G
C G A G G G A T A G C C A T T G G C
G A T C G T T C C G T C T T A T G C
T A G T T C G A A T A C A G C C A G
C A G C G A T T A C G T T A G A T C
C T C G G T G T C A A C T T A G C C
A C A C C A C T C C G A T G A C G T A
G G T A G T A C T A A G A C G C A T
G C C C T C C G A A G T C G T A T T
A C C T C C T A G C G A C T A G C G
T T G T C T A C C A G T A T C C T G
C T A T T G G T A C A A T T A C T C
G G T A T A G C A A G T C C G T A G
C A C C T A T G A G T T G A A C T T
T G C C G G G G T T A G A C G A C C
T G C A A G A T G A C G G A A A G G
A C G A A T C C A C T A A T T G C C
G A C T G C A T A C T C C A C C T G
```

1 - Stepmother, or father's wife.
2 - Step-niece.
3- Step-great-nephew.

1 4 0 2 6 9 — Jan's brother's birthday. Exactly 40 years after the St Valentine's Day Massacre, 14 February 1929

The impact appears to be caused by single, long block-shaped impact from above. The only two objects likely to have caused it are the radio and the chess clock. It seems most probable that it is from the chess clock missing from the scene. What came as a real surprise was the missing knight chess piece lodged in Holub's throat!

## PUZZLE 10

A) The landlady put the pieces back after discovering the scene because of her OCD, using her photographic memory to recall where the pieces once were. B) Jozef says he had taken "the knight", implying he had taken only one. But both are missing from the table. After questioning, it becomes apparent that the landlady could not find the knight that had been on the table, and the other had, of course, been swallowed. Her OCD left her unable to leave the table "incomplete" and so she placed a bishop where the knight had been. The missing knight was later recovered from beneath a bookcase. Jan's checkmate move was knight to f7. You might never know whether Jozef was telling the truth or not.

## PUZZLE 11

It doesn't take 30 minutes to cook chips in a deep fat fryer. It only takes about 10 minutes or less.

## PUZZLE 12

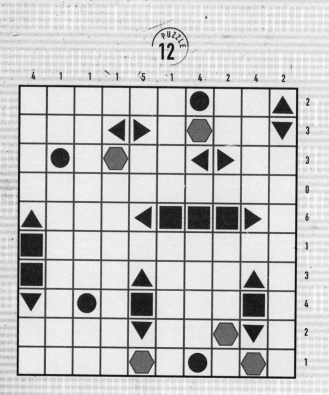

### PUZZLE 13

File 003_C_Tim Baldacci

### PUZZLE 14

The radio is out of place as there is no reception in the basement.

### PUZZLE 15

Vincent Tipton: 4 and a half beers and a fifth of two bottles of wine = 7.65+ 4 = 11.65 units.
Tim Baldacci: A vodka bottle, a quarter of a whiskey bottle and a fifth of two bottles of wine = 54 units.
Yasmin Satrapi: Quarter of a whiskey bottle, a wine box and a fifth of two bottles of wine = 54 units.
Monica Satrapi: A half-bottle of absinthe and a fifth of two bottles of wine = 55 units.
Ben Jackson = only 4 units.

### PUZZLE 16

No. Ben has no self control (3) so he is unreliable (6), so he's not calm under pressure (2), so he's not allowed a concealed pistol (4) so he never goes to major purchases (1) so he's not allowed to wear a skull-faced bandana (5).

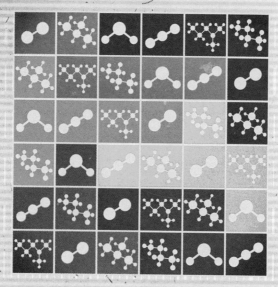

He recognised the mark in the fur around its neck.
It was the same as his girlfriend's rat used to have, and it suggests that it sometimes wears a collar.
Upon closer examination, he also spotted that it was bigger than a wild rat, as most wild rats are at most
9 to 10 inches long, while domesticated rats have longer lifespans and so can grow to up to 11 to 12
inches. He also noted its colour, as it is grey with white and brown blotches, which suggests selective
breeding. Most wild rats are just black or brown.
However, it was the collar that immediately gave it away.

1. If the rat bit the wire, it would have received a possibly deadly shock from the electricity, especially
considering the metal chip in its body. But the rat was unharmed... Unless the wire wasn't even carrying
electricity.
2. Furthermore, if the rat's biting caused a spark, it would have been caught up in the fire.
3. The bite on the wire is 5 cm, which is too large for the rat in question, as shown by the tiny 1 cm bites
taken out of the potato.
4. The wire had no fire damage, which suggests it was pulled out of the wall before the fire happened.

PUZZLE
20

1. They drank too much ipecac and were too drunk to realise they had been poisoned.
2. Tipton gave them the ipecac because he was unhappy with them constantly having parties in his basement and mocking him — Dumb Dan. He grew the ipecac plant in his herb garden.
3. Finding he had accidentally killed them, Tipton set the fire to make it seem like an accident. Beforehand he ripped the wire from the wall and clipped it to make the rat look like the likely culprit.

PUZZLE
21

The correct order is:
3. Pallor Mortis, 5. Algor Mortis, 1. Rigor Mortis, 4. Livor Mortis, 7. Putrefaction,
2. Decomposition and 6. Skeletonization.

PUZZLE
22

The bearded man's statement is NOT BELIEVABLE. His flat is too low to see anything past the staircase, and the body is not dressed in a pink bathing costume.
The tiny lady's statement is NOT BELIEVABLE. On the first floor, the railing would block her view, and being struck by lightning is very unlikely.
The dressing-gown man's statement is BELIEVABLE. On the third floor, he would have been able to see the beach.
The large-eyebrowed man's statement is NOT BELIEVABLE. The fourth floor has closed blinds, which are dusty, indicating they haven't been opened for a while. Also, his description of the assailants was very unlikely.
The pigeon man's statement is BELIEVABLE. Although his flat is on the other side, he may have been on the roof, where trained pigeons are often kept. Plus, his description agrees with that of the balding man.

PUZZLE
23

0      5      13      3

She is an off-duty police officer, probably working for the MPF (Marine Police Force) at the MSU (Marine
Support Unit) in Wapping.
Her dog is a "K9", a police dog.
She knows police jargon like SOCO.
She doesn't like being near the river due to previous incidents she's dealt with.
She uses the phrase "Oh ten hundred".
And she calls you sir.

PUZZLE
25

## PUZZLE 26

**Once reassembled the note reads:**
"I know I'm the last person you want to see but you have to meet me at 4pm tommorrow, our usual spot.
Your life depends on it. No joke!"

I know I'm the last person you want

to see but you have to meet me

at 4pm tommorrow, our usual spot.

Your life depends on it.

No joke!

## PUZZLE 27

**The compost heap is in Mr Strachan's garden next door, they have been helping him pull up dock leaf weeds and trim bushes, and they keep a plastic bin containing "food scraps" for his compost heap in the kitchen.**

## PUZZLE 28

**Wesley Bryant's and Jillian Fosdyke's handwriting both closely match the note. It is difficult to tell them apart, but Wesley has misspelled "tomorrow", which gives him away as the author.**

Can whoever keeps
taking my biscuits please
buy more tommorrow?

## PUZZLE 29

He was shot with a crossbow that used a bolt made of ice. Wesley Bryant studies history and is in a medieval re-enactment society. He's involved with crossbows, which would be able to fire an ice bolt at speed without it melting.

## PUZZLE 30

The hoard is hidden in Mr Strachan's birdhouse, which is why the magpies are nesting by the security camera. Tianka was trying to get back into the garden to retrieve the hoard. Bunch had bird faeces under his nails because he's the one who hid it there.

## PUZZLE 31

No. Not eating and smoking is good, but he threw away potential evidence, covered things in sticky tape, and moved other evidence and put it in bags without wearing protective gloves.

## PUZZLE 32

All the litter is from a barbecue place. Mr Panjit said they are all vegan by religion, so they wouldn't eat there.

## PUZZLE 33

**34**

Casa del Olivio. Olivio means "olive", as in olive oil, as was used in the bread. Harriet's Kitchen is very busy and criminals would be uncomfortable, The Poppy House is apparently full of cops, Atmos wouldn't allow you to take the bread out, and Blondini's pays too much attention to its customers.

**35**

On the brick tip jar. We know the men tipped money, and if their DNA isn't on there, it may be on the rough brick surface, which the M-Vac is able to gather DNA from.

**36**

The answer is the piston. It has two metal rings, is activated by the driver and, if the correct mixture of fuel and air isn't compressed within it, the piston won't spark.

**37**

The nine differences are circled below.

## 38

Only the first letter of each group is important. The message reads "MEET ON ROOF OF CROSSKEY".

## 39

His throat was slashed by the kite, with ground glass and razor blades glued onto its string, flown from the garden opposite.

## 40

Whatever stole the mobile from the locked room had to come through the only opening – the vent – but it knocked over the flask, scattered the test results and left some scuff marks on the wall. You surmise it could only be a drone.

## 41

A trombone was resting in the dusty patch.

| | | | | 2 | | 2 | | 4 | 2 | 2 | 2 | 4 | 5 | 7 | 9 | | | | |
| | | 2 | 2 | 2 | 8 | 4 | 2 | 5 | 8 | 2 | 2 | 2 | 2 | 2 | 2 | 2 | | | |
| | | 2 | 2 | 2 | 4 | 2 | 5 | 7 | 2 | 2 | 2 | 2 | 2 | 2 | 2 | 2 | 2 | 2 | |
| | 3 | 5 | 2 | 2 | 4 | 2 | 2 | 7 | 2 | 2 | 2 | 2 | 2 | 2 | 2 | 2 | 2 | 5 | 3 |
|---|---|---|---|---|---|---|---|---|---|---|---|---|---|---|---|---|---|---|---|
| 1 | | | | | | | | | | | | | | | | | | | |
| 2 | | | | | | | | | | | | | | | | | | | |
| 1,1,1,3 | | | | | | | | | | | | | | | | | | | |
| 1,1,1,4 | | | | | | | | | | | | | | | | | | | |
| 16 | | | | | | | | | | | | | | | | | | | |
| 17 | | | | | | | | | | | | | | | | | | | |
| 2,1,1,4 | | | | | | | | | | | | | | | | | | | |
| 2,1,1,2 | | | | | | | | | | | | | | | | | | | |
| 2,1,1,1 | | | | | | | | | | | | | | | | | | | |
| 2,1,1 | | | | | | | | | | | | | | | | | | | |
| 17 | | | | | | | | | | | | | | | | | | | |
| 17 | | | | | | | | | | | | | | | | | | | |
| 1,2 | | | | | | | | | | | | | | | | | | | |
| 1,2 | | | | | | | | | | | | | | | | | | | |
| 1,1,3 | | | | | | | | | | | | | | | | | | | |
| 2,13 | | | | | | | | | | | | | | | | | | | |
| 2,11 | | | | | | | | | | | | | | | | | | | |
| 1 | | | | | | | | | | | | | | | | | | | |

## PUZZLE 42

The five differences are circled below

## PUZZLE 43

Cyanide. There was no haemorrhaging, which eliminates arsenic. No blood was vomited and there was organ failure, which rules out ricin. The muscles did not convulse and there was no rictus grin, so not strychnine. The skin was dark red, formerly cherry, the body looked comatose, there was strain on the heart, and the lungs were filled with fluid.

## PUZZLE 44

The mobile phone is missing.

## PUZZLE 45

The Jack Russell, as that is the only dog not wearing a flea collar.

## PUZZLE 46

His voice is husky, his breath is bad and he was wearing a scarf to hide what he was nervously and subconsciously touching. The wristband he is wearing is a hospital wristband.

1. "Lucy in the Sky with Diamonds" by The Beatles,
2. "Blue Suede Shoes" by Elvis Presley,
3. "Eye of the Tiger" by Survivor,
4. "Uptown Funk" by Mark Ronson,
5. "Rock Around the Clock" by Billy Haley and The Comets

The flute track is fake because, in all other situations where the musicians are talking, bumping limbs or humming, their audio track cuts out. However, despite supposedly eating crisps, the flute's playing never cuts out.

The broken shards fit perfectly into object B — a window leading to the outside. The breakage is curious; it's not large enough for anyone to climb out of. Why would the poisoner have made it?

B

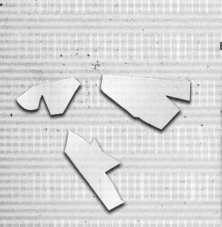

First, you must calculate the time taken to reach the ground. You know that the rocket must fall nine metres: $9 = 0.5 \times 10 \times t^2$. Thus $9 = 5t^2$, and so $t^2 = 1.8$. Therefore, the time taken to reach the ground would have been 1.34 seconds.
If the bottle rocket was travelling at 20 m/s, then it should have travelled 26.8 metres from the building before reaching the ground.

## 51

The suit tore on the spiky copper railing, which, like the statues outside, is green from verdigris.

## 52

Some kind of strong acid, for example hydrofluoric acid, was poured down from the balcony. It ate through the supports, leaving the holes and drip marks as well as the pungent, acrid smell. Hydrofluoric acid doesn't affect plastic, which is why that was unmarked.

## 53

E. This is the only plastic bin, and therefore the only one that could house the acid securely. If it was in any of the others there would be a tell-tale hole in the bottom of the bin.

## 54

The suspect is made up of A5, B3 and C6.

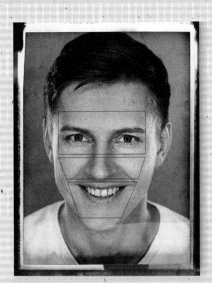

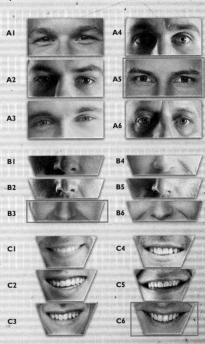

Royal Rumble is purple — purple has been associated with royalty all around the world for hundreds of years.

London Bus is red — as are the real London buses of course.

LA Nóir is black — black translates to *noir* in French.

Glistering is gold — glister is an archaic form of the word glitter, and is famously used in the *Merchant of Venice*: "All that glisters is not gold."

Ecowarrior is green — the eco movement is most closely associated with the colour green.

Therefore, Think is pink — like the Italian sportswear brand.

The suspect was kissed by Amaya.

You ask one of the AIs, "If I asked the other AI, which result would they say is true?" Whichever one they say, the other is true. This is because the lying AI will lie about what the truthful AI would say, whereas the truthful AI would tell the truth about the lying AI saying the wrong one.

A5) Inspector Hound, B2) Unibrow, C3) Piglet, D1) Pouty Pants, E4) Wookie.

The phone indicates it uses 9G, which is ridiculous because it has not yet been invented. However, you realise that it actually means 9=G, which gives you the code cipher:
A-3 B-4 C-5 D-6 E-7 F-8 G-9 H-10 I-11 J-12 K-13 L-14 M-15 N-16 O-17 P-18 Q-19 R-20 S-21 T-22 U-23 V-24 W-25 X-26 Y-1 Z-2

However, the text still does not seem to make sense. Until you realise it is all written backwards! Once you decode the text it reads:

egakcap eht teg uoy did = "Did you get the package"
suoregnad llew sti siht rof artxe teg dluohs I tub haey = "Yeah but I should get extra for this its well dangerous"
ewo uoy rebmemer ti evael ro ti ekat = "Take it or leave it remember you owe"
hguoht eid elpoep rehto tnow = "Wont other people die though"
enod ti teg taht ekil etihs yas tnod = "Don't say shite like that get it done"

**PUZZLE 59**

A. The compact and D. the map of Ibiza belong to the unfortunate Mary Pynchon, who has just returned from holiday (hence the tan lines) and wears make-up on nights out.

C. The Swiss army knife and F. the afro comb belong to Matthias Athanasiou because he has an afro hairstyle and he recently cut himself – hence the plaster on his hand. You tested the knife later and found traces of his blood on it.

Therefore, B. the key and E. the Nicaraguan residency card belong to "Bob Dobalina", whose real name is apparently Marcellino Gutierrez and, as the only person killed who was using a fake ID, may have been the target of the assassination. The key is, after some examination, revealed to be a locker key.

**PUZZLE 60**

18121999

The "1812 Overture" is a piece of music by Tchaikovsky;
"1999" is a song by Prince, which features the lyrics "Tonight I'm gonna party like it's 1999."

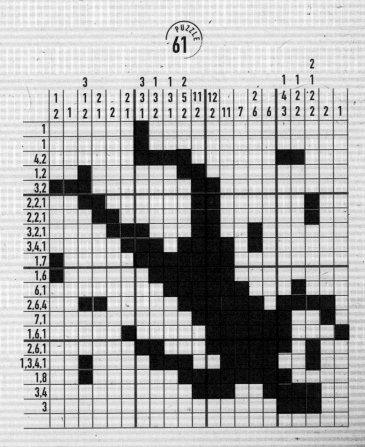

**PUZZLE 61**

**PUZZLE 62**

**PUZZLE 63**

She was probably wearing the wrong glasses when she saw the object being "dumped", as she seems confused between which glasses are which and is, in fact, wearing her reading glasses (semi-circular, half-moon, blue/periwinkle) when she meets you.

**PUZZLE 64**

The rocks float, which suggests they aren't made of stone, but plastic. They are perfectly and uniformly round, which was very difficult, if not impossible, to do in the past. One of the symbols is the yin-yang sign, which is a Chinese symbol and would not have been known or used at that time.

**PUZZLE 65**

The partial fingerprint matches that of Dan Bell.

MATCH

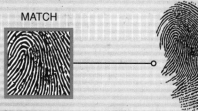

DAN BELL

## 66

It was tyre track number 8. This matched a treadmark that had been left in the mud of the dig site.
Further analysis of the mud taken from the tyre of Dan Bell's car later confirmed that his car had been on
site at some point.

## 67

Surrey is not known for earthquakes of any sort, whereas fracking is known to cause them. This
earthquake was likely caused by Middlearth fracking in the area despite the court injunction. Bell
was hired by them to go to the site and cover up any evidence of their activities, such as damage to
underground pipes.

## 68

The fish are alive and seemingly healthy. If they had been left for months, they would be dead.

## 69

Negative A matches Photo 5.
Negative B matches Photo 4.
Negative C matches Photo 1.
Negative D matches Photo 3.
Photo 2 has no negative.

## 70

It's Linus Knowles-Selman and Kit McCane, and they are married to other people. Knowles-Selman
eventually confesses he killed Matheson when he accidentally caught him *in flagrante* and tried to
blackmail him.

## 71

The polaroid has faded with time, and so is no help. However, the coins are pre-decimal, indicating the
body is from before February 1971. Led Zeppelin's debut album was released in 1969, so it is extremely
likely the body was buried sometime between 1969 and February 1971.

## 72

She's a historical fashion expert, using her knowledge of what clothing trends and fabrics were used at the time to focus in on exactly when the body was buried.

**73**

BIKINI
CULOTTES
DELARENTA
EMILIOPUCCI
GOGOBOOT
HIPPY
MARYQUANT
MINISKIRT
MOD
NICO
PACORABANNE
PAISLEY
SAINT-LAURENT
TIEDYE
TWIGGY

```
P A Z M V P N Y L D B F H S D W T B C S
G A T A K U T F L O T J K B C S S O E Y
S Q C N E I Z B M F O H D J L H H T O B
G H E O E R C X E S O E K Y F Y T R P K
I U O D R R S C X C B M U C B O J S K I
Y M Y N S A A N O E O I L R L I S F X S
M E N P C D B L I V G L S U L Y K T Y B
O T J Q N B G A E B O I C O L X U M M M
P R E R M U O F N D G O W V E S U G N M
Q G Q I Q V K W B N V P R K K X J X A I
K Z L D U S T W R Y E U P Z T Q Z R X B
T R I K S I N I M U N C J T Z O Y L G H
P A I S L E Y P I H C V U Z Q C Y S A A
U E C S O W Q O P C Y I T B U T W I F I
H N N C N S W N T M D D E A V W N W N K
D Y Y H D D Y W D J W M N H E I W I H O
S A I N T L A U R E N T D W F G H D R G
Y Y E J Y A X P N S S U O L W G X O B J
N P U D R Y Q C L W G M M Z R Y X K N A
A W E I Q P M L O L N O E C F V D U S Z
```

**74**

| First name | Surname | Age | Profession | Disappearance |
| --- | --- | --- | --- | --- |
| Ted | Spurdon | 29 | Milkman | Last seen on date |
| Bill | Thompson | 43 | Butcher | Last seen meeting supplier |
| Tom | Perrier | 18 | Gardener | Last seen at pub |
| Charlie | Palmer | 62 | Banker | Last seen at shop |
| Jack | Ryan | 39 | Policeman | Last seen on train |

**75**

Only two bets came in: Immaculate Pasta won in Race 6 with a £2 stake at 3–1, netting returns of £8. It was Race 3 where the mysterious man won a considerable sum: Phil the Flyer won on a £10 stake at 20–1, getting a return of £200 plus the £10 stake. Whoever cashed in the slip would therefore receive £218 – a considerable sum in the 1960s.

## 76

Use the genealogy databases. Spurdon died long before social media. A press release is hit-or-miss and takes time. Other departments would be in the same position as you are. You have Spurdon's DNA and the databases are full of DNA profiles from people who submit them looking for family connections.

## 77

Emily has a series of photos from her young adulthood on display, one of which shows her with Ted Spurdon. She clearly knew him well enough to keep a photo of him on display for 50 years.

## 78

Yes, because while she denies being able to name the items Cosmo shopped for, she still remembers his name, which was said at the beginning of the list.

## 79

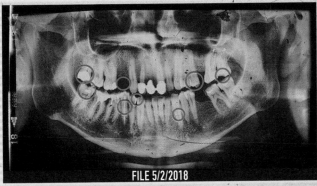

FILE 5/2/2018

## 80

She must have had an accomplice in the murder who only gave her half the money.

In their youth, Jane and Noel Terbot were actually Markus and Alice Borett, the anarchist post-office bombers. They moved to the UK to avoid capture and are still on the run. Their English surname is an anagram of their Swedish one.

The sound in the background is, bizarrely, an elephant. The taped sound must be at least as loud in each bar as the stock sound, as it contains the stock sound plus the sound of talking over the top. Therefore, the gunshot is ruled out by the third last bar of sound, and the car horn and sneeze by the final bar. Only the elephant fits.

It's a straight-six, as the sound is a "level and muted steady vibration", like a cat purring in a cardboard box.

= 18

=12

=23

=20

Therefore, the house number is 73.

The blood leads to an understairs cupboard.

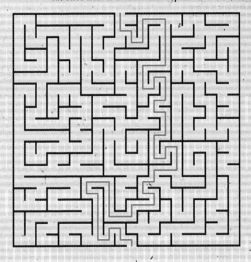

It was likely to be the tennis player, as they wore a mask of Björn Borg, their house is filled with old, tennis magazines and one arm is more muscular than the other as can happen with tennis players.

There is only one shoeprint without a pair. It is highlighted.

## PUZZLE 88

1. Sawdust = Grabbed and thrown into a builder's van.
2. Plastic fibres = Tied up at first location.
3. Grease from tyre jack = Thrown into a car boot.
4. Wet paper and ink = Tied up in the house (it was full of old magazines).
5. Blood stain = Gets cut and escapes.

## PUZZLE 89

It's a tennis racquet, not a bat. You don't score goals in tennis, you score points. There are no stumps in tennis; that's cricket. You don't get strikes in tennis; that's bowling (or baseball). It's not a pitch, it's a tennis court. You only get extra lives in computer games

## PUZZLE 90

The voice on the audio file uses the word "listen" to start sentences, as does the suspect. He also uses the unusual phrase "million of pounds" in both examples, and the term "anguish and pain".

## PUZZLE 91

1. Mr Panjit    2. SWIX    3. Vegan
4. Casa Del Olivio    5. Fyodor Bykov

Toronto is in Canada, not the United States of America.

1. Take the electromagnet through.
2. Return.
3. Take the laptop or Bridger through.
4. Return with the electromagnet.
5. Take Bridger or the laptop through.
6. Return.
7. Take the electromagnet through again.

**96**

The former medical robot also detected the angina capsules that the barrister dropped, as they contain nitro-glycerine.

**97**

You need to cut the wire that starts at the very far left-hand side of the page.

**98**

He said he used defibrillators to *give* someone a cardiac arrest, but a cardiac arrest is the same as a heart attack. You use defibrillators to treat them. Also, it's very unusual to refer to a ligament as pulled.

**99**

He has gone into the basement.

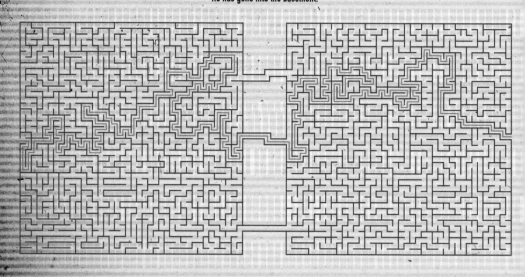

## I think it's DI Dustin Aksoy.

You take two police constables and confront Aksoy in his lab as he's surreptitiously sending an email to an unknown person.

"You're working for SW1X, aren't you?" you accuse him. "I've seen you contacting people furtively and you've been recording details of the cases and trying to involve yourself in other people's cases against their will. Come clean, Aksoy."

Aksoy looks at you and swallows. "OK, I'll confess... but not to working for SW1X. I would never work for a criminal organization! I've been secretly working... for a TV company!"

He tells you how he'd been contacted by the makers of a new TV show about forensic detectives, and how they wanted inside information about what it was like. He didn't have permission and was worried he wouldn't get it, so he lied and told them he could provide them with all the information they needed.

"I was just so excited about being involved in TV! The glitz, the glamour... Did you know my mum named me after Dustin Hoffman? But I know what I did was wrong. I broke the prime directive."

You report Aksoy to his bosses but, although what he's done is inappropriate, he is not the traitor.

## I think it's DI Abigail Beckhoff.

You're not sure where Beckhoff is in the building but you know she's in here somewhere. On a hunch, you go to the door that she told you led to a room filled with asbestos. It's locked but, after a couple of police officers smash the lock, you open the door to find... another lab!

Beckhoff and a man you've never seen before are in the middle of testing unfamiliar-looking evidence and you step forward.

"You're working for SWIX aren't you?" you accuse her. "You have a secret lab here that no one else knows about. They got to you because of your brother's debts..."

Beckhoff shakes her head. "No. If you think I'd work for SWIX, you have no idea about me. This isn't a lab for them. This is work for... private companies."

Beckhoff outlines it to you as the other man stands awkwardly nearby. She did need money to help pay off her brother's debts, and was aware that there were rooms and equipment going unused due to the downsizing of the department. She realized she could do work for private companies on the side to make extra cash, but had to keep it secret as she found it unlikely the bosses would sign off on it.

The man is a technician she hired; a civilian. "But he's never been anywhere near any of our criminal cases. I've been very careful. I'm an excellent planner."

You report Beckhoff to her superiors — this is a very serious offense. But she's not the traitor.

### I think it's DI Kelvin Kempster.

Kempster greets you warmly as you enter his lab. "Ah, excellent. You can help me with this blood analysis…"

Then his face turns a little darker when he sees the two policemen behind you. "I see. It's like that, is it?"

With a flourish, he throws an entire tray of samples at the three of you! As you react, he pushes past you in the doorway and desperately runs for the exit, only to have his way barred by the other two officers you'd positioned there. In a panic, he runs for the stairwell, and pretty soon, he's up on the roof, cornered by you and the other officers, brandishing his trophy for Pathologist of the Year like an ineffectual weapon.

"Lovely weather!" he says of the lashing rain. "Let's hope no one flies a kite, eh?"

Then his expression turns serious. "OK. You've got your traitor. It was me. Happy?"

He tells you of how SW1X used his need for success to get to him, plied him with money and influence, and got him to interfere with the cases, using his position as the team's number-one pathologist to skew the results of cases. But he found it much more difficult when you arrived, and when Vernon got Operation Guineafowl, your involvement meant he got too close to the truth and Kempster had to arrange to have him murdered.

"I couldn't operate under your scrutiny! I tried to prejudice the balcony-collapse case. I tried to frame the fracking employee for that murder. Did you know the archaeologist was smuggling items for SW1X? That's what they do; they find people who are greedy or impressionable or just stupid, like the courtroom bomber, and they twist them. Like they twisted me!"

He steps a little closer to the edge of the roof. You all move forward carefully.

"But that's not the half of it. SW1X aren't based in Kensington! Stupid name to cover a very clever organization. It should be called SW1A! They're all police, and it goes right to the top. I've got it all – names, dates, everything – on a memory stick. But it won't do me any good."

He puts the trophy down carefully. "I'm sorry."

And then he leaps 10 storeys to his death.

To: deaddrop73@secureserve.org.ch
From: CS.Bill.Stoneman@met.police.uk

Subject: Operation Barrow

So it was Kempster. Good riddance to bad rubbish. The department is severely compromised but at least we got the rotter.

I see you omitted from your report all that nonsense he talked on the roof about SW1X having anything to do with coppers. I hope that means you recognize that it was completely baseless. If he'd had any evidence about it, he probably would have given it to you, wouldn't he?

On an unrelated note, you don't know what happened to his trophy for Pathologist of the Year, do you? His widow wanted it – sentimental value, I think.

I hope that you're ready to move on from this case and onto something different. You've got a bright future ahead of you and you don't seem the type to do anything silly like accusing your superiors of running an organized-crime syndicate from inside the police.

...Are you?

-Bill

*Bill*

**ARE YOU?**